THE CAMBRIDGE BIBLE COMMENTARY

NEW ENGLISH BIBLE

GENERAL EDITORS

P. R. ACKROYD, A. R. C. LEANEY, J. W. PACKER

JOHN

THE
GOSPEL ACCORDING TO
JOHN

COMMENTARY BY

A. M. HUNTER

Professor of New Testament in the University of Aberdeen

CAMBRIDGE

AT THE UNIVERSITY PRESS

1965

PUBLISHED BY
THE SYNDICS OF THE CAMBRIDGE UNIVERSITY PRESS

Bentley House, 200 Euston Road, London, N.W. 1
American Branch: 32 East 57th Street, New York 22, N.Y.
West African Office: P.O. Box 33, Ibadan, Nigeria

©

CAMBRIDGE UNIVERSITY PRESS

1965

220.77
C178
1965
v.43

GENERAL EDITORS' PREFACE

The aim of this series is to provide the text of the New English Bible closely linked to a commentary in which the results of modern scholarship are made available to the general reader. Teachers and young people preparing for such examinations as the General Certificate of Education at Ordinary or Advanced Level in Britain, and similar qualifications elsewhere have been especially kept in mind. The commentators have been asked to assume no specialized theological knowledge, and no knowledge of Greek and Hebrew. Bare references to other literature and multiple references to other parts of the Bible have been avoided. Actual quotations have been given as often as possible.

Within these quite severe limits each commentator will attempt to set out the main findings of recent New Testament scholarship, and to describe the historical background to the text. The main theological content of the New Testament will also be critically discussed.

Much attention has been given to the form of the volumes. The aim is to produce books each of which will be read consecutively from first to last page. The introductory material leads naturally into the text, which itself leads into the alternating sections of commentary. By this means it is hoped that each book will be easily read and remain in the mind as a unity.

The series will be prefaced by a volume—*Understanding the New Testament*—which will outline the larger historical background, say something about the growth and transmission of the text, and answer the question 'Why should we study the New Testament?' Another volume—*The New Testament Illustrated*—will contain maps, diagrams and photographs.

P. R. A.
A. R. C. L.
J. W. P.

CONTENTS

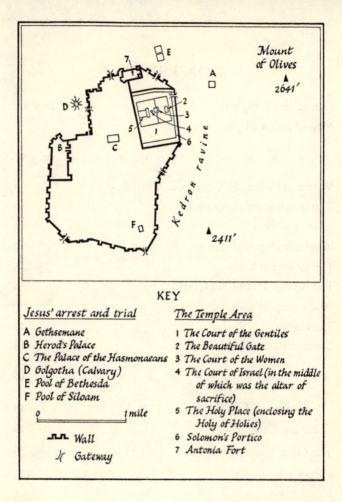

KEY

Jesus' arrest and trial

A Gethsemane
B Herod's Palace
C The Palace of the Hasmonaeans
D Golgotha (Calvary)
E Pool of Bethesda
F Pool of Siloam

0 ————————— 1 mile

ⅢⅢ Wall

)(Gateway

The Temple Area

1 The Court of the Gentiles
2 The Beautiful Gate
3 The Court of the Women
4 The Court of Israel (in the middle
   of which was the altar of
   sacrifice)
5 The Holy Place (enclosing the
   Holy of Holies)
6 Solomon's Portico
7 Antonia Fort

PLAN OF THE TEMPLE

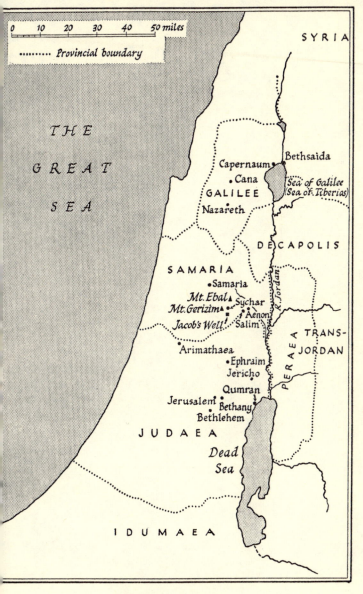

0   10   20   30   40   50 miles

.... *Provincial boundary*

SYRIA

THE

GREAT

SEA

Capernaum •   Bethsaida

• Cana

GALILEE   *Sea of Galilee*
           (Sea of Tiberias)

Nazareth •

DECAPOLIS

SAMARIA

• Samaria

Mt. Ebal ▲
Mt. Gerizim ▲ Sychar

          • Aenon
Jacob's Well ! Salim

       PERAEA   TRANS-

• Arimathaea   JORDAN

     • Ephraim
     Jericho

     Qumran

Jerusalem •
     • Bethany
   Bethlehem

JUDAEA

*Dead
Sea*

IDUMAEA

MAP OF PALESTINE

ix

THE GOSPEL ACCORDING TO
JOHN

In order to read a New Testament book intelligently, we must know, if possible, who wrote it, where, when, why and for whom. The first of these questions we will leave to the end, because it is far from simple, and consider first some of the other important problems.

WHERE AND WHEN THE GOSPEL WAS WRITTEN

Where was the Gospel written? Some have guessed Antioch, others Alexandria; but by far the strongest claim belongs to Ephesus in Asia, so that John's Gospel is often called 'the Ephesian Gospel'. The claim rests on the testimony of Irenaeus (Bishop of Lyons *c.* 180) who had known the aged Polycarp, the personal friend of the Apostle John and others who had seen Jesus. This is what Irenaeus says: 'John, the disciple of the Lord, who leaned on his breast, himself issued the Gospel while dwelling in Ephesus' and he adds that John lived there 'till the times of Trajan' (98–117).

This long residence of the Apostle in Ephesus is asserted or implied by a number of early Christian writers, including Justin Martyr and Polycrates (who had both lived in Ephesus). Some very late and dubious evidence that the Apostle died an early martyr's death should be rejected.

When was it written? The discovery in 1920 of a papyrus fragment of the Gospel (now one of the chief treasures of the John Rylands Library in Manchester) proves that the Gospel was circulating in Egypt about A.D. 130, and must—if we allow a generation for the book to travel from Ephesus—have been written not later than A.D. 100. How early we date it depends on whether we think 'John' knew the Gospels of Mark and Luke. If he knew them, the Gospel's date can hardly be earlier than 90. If he did not—as more and more scholars believe—we may date the Gospel as early as 80, perhaps even earlier. But the traditions about Jesus in the Gospel must of course be a good deal earlier.

THE LANGUAGE OF THE GOSPEL

In what language was the Gospel originally written? The answer is: Greek—though one or two scholars have argued for Aramaic (a Semitic tongue resembling Hebrew). John obviously had Greek readers in mind. This is why he translates Hebrew and Aramaic words (Siloam, Gabbatha, Golgotha, etc.) for the benefit of his readers, and why he is at pains to explain Jewish religious practices and burial customs.

Yet, if he did write in Greek, the presence in his style of many Aramaic idioms (not of course now traceable in the idiomatic English of the N.E.B.) strongly suggests that his mother-tongue was Aramaic. This is something to be remembered when we come to discuss the Gospel's authorship.

ITS ARRANGEMENT

Do we have the Gospel in its original order? Fifty years ago scholars had a craze for rearranging the chapters of the Gospel. An example of this rearrangement will be found in Dr Moffatt's translation of the New Testament. This was not merely the scholars' wilfulness. Scribes may have displaced passages when copying manuscripts. Moreover, it is undeniable that if we reverse (say) the order of chapters 5 and 6 we seem to improve the geography of Jesus' movements. Yet all such rearranging implies that we know the order John intended—a pretty big assumption. We must not confuse 'feelings' about the right order with 'proof' of it.

Significantly, most recent scholars call a halt to this reshuffling; and we do not feel justified in doing any in this book.

ITS RELATIONSHIP WITH THE SYNOPTIC GOSPELS

What is the relation of John to Matthew, Mark and Luke? It has long been recognized that in many ways John stands apart from the first three Gospels, commonly called 'Synoptic' (because they exhibit a common outline of Jesus' ministry). What are these differences?

(1) In the Synoptics, Jesus' ministry is located in Galilee with but one recorded journey to Jerusalem in the south. In John, Jesus makes several visits—generally at festival times —to Judaea and Jerusalem. Indeed, though John records the Galilean ministry, he also records an earlier Judaean ministry and a later Judaean one (after the Galilean one is over).

(2) On one or two points of chronology John diverges from the first three Gospels. Thus, he sets the cleansing of the Temple at the beginning of Jesus' ministry (not at the end, as in the Synoptics); and he dates the crucifixion a day earlier than the others.

(3) John does not chronicle certain important episodes found in the Synoptics—the Baptism of Jesus and the Temptation, the Transfiguration, the institution of the Lord's Supper, the Agony in the Garden. On the other hand, he has various new stories to tell about Jesus—the dialogues with Nicodemus and the Samaritan woman, Jesus' activity in Jerusalem from the feast of Tabernacles to that of Dedication (7–10), the raising of Lazarus, the foot-washing, the inquiry before Annas, besides certain appearances of the risen Lord.

(4) Like the Synoptics, John declares that Jesus wrought miracles, recording in fact seven of them; but he calls them 'signs' (not 'mighty works', as in the Synoptics); and he always stresses their spiritual meaning by following up the 'work' with an explanatory saying or 'word'.

(5) Instead of the short, pithy sayings and numerous parables

found on Jesus' lips in the Synoptics, John ascribes to Jesus long discourses whose themes are life, light, truth, judgement, Christ's person and his relation to the Father.

(6) On certain points of theology John seems to diverge from the Synoptics. Thus, in the Synoptics the main theme of Jesus' preaching is 'the kingdom of God', in John it is 'eternal life'. Again, whereas in the very first chapter of John men acclaim Jesus as Messiah, it is well on in the ministry, according to Mark, before this happens.

Are these differences real and serious? Once the argument was that if John disagreed with the Synoptics, we should distrust his testimony. To follow the Synoptics, said the critics, was the way of wisdom. Nowadays we realize not only that these differences are *overdrawn* but that often, where they do exist, John is to be followed. Here are a few examples.

Not only do the Synoptics drop unwitting hints that Jesus visited Jerusalem more than once in his ministry, but many scholars are convinced that there was, as John records, a Judaean ministry before the Galilean one began, and a later ministry in the south after the Galilean one was over.

Many believe that John is right about the date of the Last Supper.

Though John does not record Jesus' Baptism, the institution of the Lord's Supper, and the Agony in the Garden, he shows quite clearly that he knew about them (1: 32; 6: 51; 12: 27).

The distinction between the Synoptics' treatment of the miracles as 'mighty works' and John's treatment as 'signs' has been too sharply drawn. Closer study shows that even in the first three Gospels Jesus' mighty works are 'signs'—for those who have eyes to see.

Nor is it true to say that the Jesus of John's Gospel always speaks in long discourses and without parables. There are at least half-a-dozen parables, and some sixty short pointed sayings like those found in the Synoptics, e.g. 3: 3, 'unless a man has been born over again he cannot see the kingdom of God'.

4

Finally, a passage like Matt. 11: 27, 'Everything is entrusted to me by my Father; and no one knows the Son but the Father, and no one knows the Father but the Son and those to whom the Son may choose to reveal him'—so reminiscent of much in John's Gospel—warns us against the unwisdom of magnifying the theological differences between John and the Synoptics.

Nonetheless, the differences being what they are, the question arises: Did John know the earlier Gospels?

Not so very long ago the unanimous answer was: Yes, John knew Mark and probably Luke. The case for John's knowledge of Mark rested chiefly on his apparent borrowing of phrases from Mark in the stories of the feeding of the multitude (e.g. 'twenty pounds of bread') and the anointing at Bethany (e.g. 'oil of pure nard'). Verbal points of contact in their references to Martha and Mary suggested that John also knew Luke. But odd verbal coincidences like these can naturally be explained by the theory that (say) the story of Jesus' anointing was current in the oral tradition of the Gospels and that both John and Mark, quite independently, got their accounts of it there. This, plus the fact that where they are recounting the same story, John and Mark show such striking differences in the telling of it, has led many modern scholars to deny John's dependence on the Synoptics outright.

THE GOSPEL AS HISTORY

If John is independent of the first three Gospels, what is the historical value of his story of Jesus?

At one time—and not long ago—it was the fashion among scholars to 'take a poor view' of John as history. How considerably they have revised their opinions in the light of advancing knowledge may be illustrated by the judgement of one of the greatest of them: 'There is a growing body of evidence,' wrote T. W. Manson, 'that the Fourth Gospel enshrines a tradition of the Ministry which is independent of the Synoptic accounts, bears distinct marks of its Palestinian origin, and is on some points quite possibly superior to the Synoptic record.'

The point is worth illustrating.

A comparison of the sequence of events in John 6 (the feeding, the walking on the water, the return to the west side of the Lake, Peter's Confession) with its counterpart in Mark 6–8, shows that John's whole account hangs together as a unit and may fairly claim to be historically superior to Mark's.

This is only one of several possible comparisons. If this is so, the presumption is that in other passages, not paralleled in the first three Gospels, we are handling trustworthy traditions. To this presumption we may add a practical test. Where something recorded by John only helps to make sense of the story of Jesus as we know it from the Synoptics, it has a fair claim to be reckoned authentic. Thus:

> John alone tells us that two of Jesus' disciples had previously followed John the Baptist (1: 35 ff.).
> John testifies to a Judaean ministry before the Galilean one (3: 22 ff.).
> John tells us that after the feeding of the multitude a Messianic uprising seemed imminent (6: 15).
> John testifies that there was a later ministry, lasting some months, in the south and before the Passion (7: 10 — 11: 54).
> John records that Jesus appeared informally before Annas, the ex High Priest, after his arrest (18: 13 ff.).

On each of these points we may reasonably suppose John to be right.

If now we turn from John's history to his geography, there is the same tale to tell. Once it was the fashion to treat John's notes about topography with grave suspicion. Now, at place after place—Aenon near Salim, Bethesda, Gabbatha, etc.—the archaeologists have proved him right. Nor is this all. Most of the place-names which occur only in John belong to southern Palestine; while Galilean place-names common in

the Synoptics—Chorazin, Caesarea Philippi, Decapolis, etc.
—do not occur. It looks as if John's special traditions about
Jesus were associated with southern Palestine—another point
to remember when we discuss the matter of authorship.

Consider next the sayings set on Jesus' lips by John. Once
men like Matthew Arnold declared that if Jesus spoke as he
does in the first three Gospels, he could not have spoken as
John represents him in the fourth. Three reasons may be noted
why we cannot now endorse this extreme judgement.

(1) Very often the teaching of Jesus in John's Gospel is expressed in the same poetic forms as we find in the first three.
Jesus' dialogue with Nicodemus, for example, has sayings like

'That which is born of the flesh is flesh:
That which is born of the Spirit is spirit' (3: 6)

which show that parallelism, or 'rhyming of thoughts', which
marks Jesus' teaching in, say, the Sermon on the Mount in
Matthew.

(2) Many 'Johannine' sayings of Jesus are at once so
reminiscent of, yet different from, sayings in the Synoptics
that quite obviously John had access to a tradition of Jesus'
teaching independent of the earlier Gospels. For example:

'The man who loves himself is lost, but he who hates
himself in this world will be kept safe for eternal life' (12: 25).

There are many more like this in John. Now, such evidence
makes it likely that some sayings *found only in* John are no less
genuine. In fact, some are so clearly 'uninventable' that they
must be genuine; for example 5: 17: 'My Father has never
yet ceased his work, and I am working too', a saying which
flatly contradicts the statement in Gen. 2: 3 that God rested
from his work on the seventh day.

(3) In *A Death in the Desert* Browning makes the dying
Apostle John say,

What first were guessed as points I now knew stars
And named them in the Gospel I have writ.

7

This exactly describes much that we find in John—'points' in the earlier Gospel tradition which have become 'stars' in the Fourth Gospel. Thus, Jesus' claim to unique Sonship in Matt. 11:27 (already quoted) is elaborated in such 'Johannine' sayings as these:

'The Father loves the Son and has entrusted him with all authority' (3: 35);
'the Father knows me and I know the Father' (10: 15).

Or, again, the five sayings in John about the Holy Spirit seem to amplify sayings of Jesus about the Spirit in the earlier Gospels. This, again, is a point which could be abundantly illustrated.

If these Johannine sayings of Jesus often bear the marks of John's own style and of Christian experience, they should be regarded not as John's 'inventions' but as 'inspired paraphrases', made under the Spirit's influence, of what Jesus really said. 14: 25 f. probably supplies the true clue: 'I have told you all this while I am still here with you; but your Advocate, the Holy Spirit whom the Father will send in my name, will teach you everything, and will call to mind all that I have told you.'

In John's version of Jesus' teaching we have to reckon with three elements: (1) the sayings of Jesus—'I have told you all this'; (2) the memory of the disciples—'will call to mind'; and (3) the interpreting Spirit—'will teach you everything'. Only those who take a low view of the Spirit's guidance of the Church will regret the presence of the third element in John's record of Jesus' teaching.

THE BACKGROUND OF THE GOSPEL

Is the background of John's Gospel Jewish or Greek? Not long ago it was commonly held that in John we see the Gospel beginning to be changed by its contact with Greek thought; and scholars set out to prove that John's thinking was like that of Philo the Hellenistic Jew of Alexandria (20 B.C. to A.D. 50) or resembled the Greek Hermetic literature, i.e. mystical writings, purporting to give knowledge of God, produced in Egypt between A.D. 100 and 200. On the other hand, his debt to the Old Testament and, in places, to the Jewish rabbis seemed no less clear. Was John then equally indebted to Jew and Greek?

If nowadays most of us would stress the basic Jewishness of John's Gospel, it is because of the discovery in 1947 (and later) of the Dead Sea Scrolls. Down at Qumran, on the north-western shore of the Dead Sea, we have uncovered evidence of members of a Jewish sect who thought and spoke in terms very like John's. Anybody who reads one of these Scrolls, called *The Manual of Discipline* (which sets forth the rules of the sect), will not have gone far before he lights on the very ungreek phrase 'to do the truth' (John 3: 21). A little later, an allusion to 'the light of life' will recall John 8: 12. Further on, the *Manual's* words about creation—

By his knowledge everything has been brought into being,
And everything that is, he established by his purpose,
And apart from him, nothing is done

will ring another bell in his memory (John 1: 3). Above all, he will find parallels in the Scrolls to John's great contrasts between light and darkness, truth and error, spirit and flesh. And he will be forced to conclude that, for the most part, we do not need to look beyond Palestine for the soil in which John's theology grew.

To say this is not to deny that John sometimes borrowed words like *Logos* (=word) belonging to the religious vocabulary of the Hellenistic world around him. This, after all, is only what we should have expected from one living in a city like Ephesus. But it is to assert that the basic background of the Gospel is Jewish and Palestinian.

When we try to assess its Christian background, three things need to be said.

First, as C. H. Dodd has shown in his *Apostolic Preaching*, behind John's Gospel, as behind the earlier ones, stands the earliest preached Gospel, or *kerygma* (= the message proclaimed).

Second, the view once held that John was, spiritually speaking, a disciple of Paul, will no longer hold. We can hardly imagine a disciple of Paul who has nothing to say about Christ as the Second Adam and never once uses the verb 'justify', or the phrase 'the righteousness of God'.

Ultimately, of course, the central figure behind John's Gospel is Jesus Christ—at once 'the Jesus of history' and 'the Christ of faith'—as he lived and wrought in the soul of the evangelist by the power of the promised Spirit.

JOHN'S PURPOSE AND AUDIENCE

Why and for whom did John write his Gospel? 20: 31 appears to provide the answer: 'Those [signs] here written have been recorded in order that you may hold the faith that Jesus is the Christ, the Son of God, and that through this faith you may possess eternal life by his name.' But instead of 'hold the faith' some manuscripts read here 'come to believe'. Did then John write to confirm believers in their faith or to win unbelievers to the faith? Perhaps he had both aims. But this verse by itself will not answer our question. We must consider the character of the Gospel as a whole.

One or two modern scholars have thought that John designed his Gospel as 'a missionary tract for the Jews of the Dispersion' (i.e. the many Jews scattered about in the world outside Palestine). But this view does not account for John's practice of explaining Jewish festivals and religious practices for the benefit of his readers who would not have needed such explanations if they were Jews, or his presentation of the chief gift of the Gospel as 'eternal life'—a subject which would certainly interest Gentiles quite as much as Jews. That he had in mind the needs of the religiously minded public in and around Ephesus—non-Christians as well as Christians —seems clear if we take his book as a whole.

What he does in it, whether deliberately or not, is to *interpret* the story of Jesus as we know it from the earlier Gospel tradition. In the cosmopolitan world of Ephesus there must have been many interested in the Christian faith but unfamiliar with Jewish terms like 'the kingdom of God' (only twice mentioned in the Gospel): people who were asking other, and more searching, questions about Jesus and the Gospel. What place did Jesus hold in the saving ways of God with men? What was the chief blessing which the Gospel offered to men? And how did Jesus remain a living and vital force in the world? There is no doubt that in his book John does supply answers to these questions.

May we then say that John's aim was to bring out for his readers—Jews and Greeks alike—the abiding significance of the tradition about Jesus already familiar in the churches? Even in the first three Gospels certain episodes are attempts to convey absolute and eternal truth, for example, the stories of the Baptism and the Transfiguration, with their suggestions of the heavenly world breaking through into this one. But they occur here and there—like breaks in the cloud which give us fleeting glimpses of the infinite blue vault of heaven. What John did in his Gospel was to show the whole story of Jesus in this way—as the place in history where the ultimate truth of God is to be found. For John, the story is 'an earthly story'—and he has no patience with those who deny its earthliness, as some heretics were evidently doing (see the First Letter of John)—but 'an earthly story with a heavenly meaning' (as the old definition of a parable put it). The 'heavenly meaning', however, is not something capriciously imposed on a plain tale which could be better told without it. It is the true meaning of the earthly story. And the proof of this lies in the fact that John's Gospel does make sense of the earlier Gospel tradition. In fact, as Calvin and many others have found, the Fourth Gospel is a key which opens the door to the understanding of the first three. What John has done for countless Christians down nineteen centuries must have been part, and the main part, of his purpose when he sat down to write, some time in the last quarter of the first.

THE AUTHOR

We come at last to the question, Who was 'John'? Let us briefly marshal the evidence and see where it leads.

(1) A second-century tradition (already mentioned) whose chief witness is Irenaeus affirms that the Apostle John lived to a ripe old age in Ephesus and 'issued' the Gospel there. To be sure, there is some evidence, from five or more centuries later, that the son of Zebedee was martyred early by the Jews. But since under examination it proves to be worthless, we may judge the case for John's having lived in Ephesus to be strong.

(2) Not so convincing is the case for his actual authorship. The earliest evidence for it is the claim made (by the elders of Ephesus?) in John 21: 24 that 'the disciple whom Jesus loved' (verse 20) wrote the Gospel. But *he wrote it* may mean, as it does in 19: 19, 'he caused it to be written'.

The case is weakened by the fact that towards the end of the second century heretics called the *Alogi* ('the Logos-less', a contemptuous nickname given them because by their rejection of the Gospel of the *Logos* they showed themselves without *logos* 'reason', i.e. stupid) and some others refused to accept John's Gospel. Would they have done so if it were common knowledge that the Gospel was an Apostle's work?

(3) With the external evidence indecisive, let us turn to the internal, asking first, Who was the Beloved Disciple?

Among many guesses, only one is probable—John the Apostle, son of Zebedee. Two reasons may be given. (*a*) Except in 21: 2, the son of Zebedee is not mentioned in the Gospel. A very odd state of affairs—unless in fact his name is hidden in the phrase 'the disciple whom Jesus loved'.

(*b*) Only the Twelve were present at the Last Supper. Of the Twelve the three closest to Christ were Peter, James and John, 'elect of the elect'. Of these three Peter is clearly distinguished from the Beloved Disciple (13: 23 f.); and James had been slain by King Herod about A.D. 44—many years before the Gospel could have been written.

(4) We may now attempt a solution to the problem. The external evidence, although supporting the Apostle John's residence in Ephesus, does not prove he wrote the Gospel. The internal evidence seems against it: (*a*) Would the Apostle have been likely to style himself his Master's 'favourite pupil'? Surely not. (*b*) Surely the son of Zebedee would have recorded the sayings of Jesus in a form more like that which we find in the earlier Gospels?

On the other hand, the Gospel contains so many signs of being written by an eyewitness (cf. 1: 14 and 19: 35), so manifestly preserves an excellent historical tradition about Jesus, and speaks with so firm a note of apostolic authority that we are driven to find a close connexion between it and the Apostle John.

The solution which does best justice to all the facts is that the actual author was himself a close disciple of the Apostle John, the Beloved Disciple.

Of this man we can affirm (1) that his very accurate Palestinian topography, his knowledge of Jewish customs and his Jewish-sounding Greek point strongly to an Aramaic-speaking Jew who had lived the first part of his life in Palestine before he settled in Ephesus, probably before A.D. 66 when Rome began the conquest of Judaea: and (2) that if style and theology are any guides, he was 'the Elder' (2 John 1: 1, 3 John 1) who wrote the three Letters of John.

Who was 'the Elder'? Papias, bishop of Hierapolis (A.D. 60–130), knew of two eminent Johns in the early Church: one John the Apostle, and the other 'the Elder John'. Moreover, according to tradition there were two tombs in Ephesus bearing the name of John. Not unreasonably many conclude that 'the Elder John' was the Fourth Evangelist and the disciple of the Apostle John. If this be so, our book is the Gospel of John the Elder according to the teaching of John the Apostle.

CONTENT AND SIGNIFICANCE

Here is a short analysis of the Gospel's contents:

The greatness of this Gospel is beyond all dispute. All down the centuries countless Christians, high and humble, have recognized it for what it is, a statement of the Gospel in its most permanent and universal form. Luther spoke for many. 'Never in my life,' he said, 'have I read a book written in simpler words than this, and yet the words are inexpressible.'

Here in words and symbols which come home to men in every age is set forth the ultimate meaning of the blessed thing God did for our sin-sick world when he gave his only Son for its saving. Nor do the ancient truths lose their spiritual magic and power when they are reincarnated in the English of the New English Bible: as witness—

the nature of God: *God is spirit, and those who worship him must worship in spirit and in truth.*

the meaning of the 'Fact of Christ': *the Word became flesh; he came to dwell among us, and we saw his glory.*

the purpose of the Incarnation and Atonement: *God loved the world so much that he gave his only Son, that everyone who has faith in him may not die but have eternal life.*

and the Christian Hope: *There are many dwelling-places in*

my Father's house...I am going there on purpose to prepare a place for you...so that where I am you may be also.

It is small wonder that this Gospel remains to this day 'the text-book of the parish priest and the inspiration of the straightforward layman' (Hoskyns). 'Go, read where I first cast my anchor,' said the dying John Knox to his wife, and without further instruction she turned to the seventeenth chapter of John. That spiritual anchorage is still available, for all who would have it, in this the profoundest of the Gospels.

✲ ✲ ✲ ✲ ✲ ✲ ✲ ✲ ✲ ✲ ✲ ✲ ✲

The Coming of Christ

THE PROLOGUE

WHEN ALL THINGS began, the Word already was. **1**
The Word dwelt with God, and what God was, the
Word was. The Word, then, was with God at the 2
beginning, and through him all things came to be; no 3
single thing was created without him. All that came to be
was alive with his life, and that life was the light of men. 4
The light shines on in the dark, and the darkness has never 5
quenched it.

✲ No book ever opened more magnificently. Mark begins his story of Jesus at Jordan, Matthew and Luke start in Bethlehem. But John goes back to the very beginning of history, even beyond it, as if to say, 'There is only one true perspective in which to see the story—you must see it in the light of eternity'.

When all things began is the N.E.B.'s equivalent of the A.V.'s 'in the beginning'. The Greek *en archē*, echoing Gen. 1: 1, means 'at the beginning of history'. John begins a new Genesis story: this one is to be about him who is the revealer of God. To a Greek who knew nothing of Genesis the words could also signify 'in principle'—at the heart of the universe. So too with the Greek *Logos* translated *Word*. To a Jew, the Word of God meant first the creative power of God in action. 'God *said*, Let there be light: and there *was* light.' Then it meant the guiding purpose of God at work in history, especially Hebrew history. Thus the Word of God came to an Amos or an Isaiah, and the course of history was given a new meaning, a new direction. It could also stand for the care and kindness of God: 'He sendeth his word, and healeth them' (Ps. 107: 20). To a Jew therefore the Word meant God showing himself in his power, wisdom and love. On the other hand, to a Greek, especially if he had read the Stoic philosophers, the *Logos* meant the Rational Principle permeating all reality. If John was seeking common ground with all possible readers, perhaps he meant both. Besides, he needed a term which would go straight to the heart of reality. For both Jew and Greek, *Logos* was just the term he wanted. For it meant the ruling fact of the universe, and that fact as the self-expression of God. So John said, *When all things began, the Word already was.*

But he said more: *the Word dwelt with God.* Its essence was a personal relation—*and what God was, the Word was*—its nature was that of God himself. So, briefly and majestically, John affirms the pre-existence, the personality and the divinity of the Word.

With verse 3 we pass from the thought of the Divine life to that of creation. So far from the universe being eternal, we learn, it is God's creation through his agent, the Divine Word: *no single thing was created without him.*

This statement of course raises the problem of evil. If a good God created everything, where does evil come from? The reference in verse 5 to the *darkness* in the world shows that John was not unaware of it, and later he will show us the incarnate Word, Jesus Christ, taking deadly but victorious issue with it in the cross.

With verses 4 f. John proceeds to tell how the Divine Word was the source of life as well as the agent of creation. *All that came to be was alive with his life, and that life was the light of men.* *Life* means quickening power, *light* moral and spiritual illumination. Both are key-words in John. Of what time is he thinking in these verses? Hardly yet of the Christian era, though the statement *the light shines on in the dark* would fit it also. The reference is rather to Old Testament times when the light of God's revelation to Israel pierced the darkness of surrounding heathenism, like a lighthouse on a headland throwing its radiant beam into 'the encircling gloom'. *And the darkness has never quenched it.* Good as the N.E.B.'s *quenched* is, 'mastered' would be better, for the Greek verb *katelaben* admits two meanings: 'did not overcome' and 'did not understand it'. John probably meant both. ✳

There appeared a man named John, sent from God; he came as a witness to testify to the light, that all might become believers through him. He was not himself the light; he came to bear witness to the light. The real light which enlightens every man was even then coming into the world.

He was in the world; but the world, though it owed its being to him, did not recognize him. He entered his own realm, and his own would not receive him. But to all who did receive him, to those who have yielded him their allegiance, he gave the right to become children of God, not born of any human stock, or by the fleshly desire of a human father, but the offspring of God himself. So the Word became flesh; he came to dwell among us, and we saw his glory, such glory as befits the Father's only Son, full of grace and truth.

[marginal verse numbers: 6, 7, 8, 9, 10, 11, 12, 13, 14]

＊ Poetry gives way to prose as we hear now of the prepara-
tion, in the Baptist's mission, for the final Revelation. *There
appeared a man named John, sent from God.* How abruptly
John the Baptist makes his entry! Whereas the Word *was*
(eternally), John arose, like some Hebrew judge or prophet,
at God's summons. If we want to know what John looked
like and what he taught, we must go back to the earlier
Gospels. In this Gospel he is essentially a pointing figure, a
witness to the greater One, the Messiah. *Not himself the light*
(had some of John's disciples made excessive claims for their
master?) he came to bear witness to it.

And now (verse 9) with the Baptist's appearance, the hour
of revelation is near. We should say that Jesus of Nazareth
stood on the threshold of his ministry. But John (the evangelist) who sees 'the Fact of Christ' in its eternal significance, says:
*The real light which enlightens every man was even then coming
into the world* (verse 9). Even as the Baptist was bearing his
witness, there was entering the world that light in whose
radiance all others seem dim, the light which can make clear
to every man the meaning of his life and destiny.

With deep pathos verses 10 and 11 tell what happened at
the Incarnation. In the world to which he came, God's agent
in its creation went unrecognized. When he *entered his own
realm* (or 'his own home'), i.e. Israel as the natural home of
the true light, his own folk refused to welcome him. On this
statement the best commentary is Jesus' own parable of the
wicked vine-growers (Mark 12: 1–9).

Yet (verse 12) some received him, and to them he gave the
right, or privilege, of becoming members of God's family.
Note that John calls believers *children of God*, reserving the
title 'Son' for Christ. These were the people who *yielded him
their allegiance*. In the Greek, this is literally 'believed in his
name'. But since 'name' means 'revealed character' and
'believe in' expresses personal trust, the phrase signifies those
who confessed Jesus to be Son of God. These children of the
new divine birth—a theme to be developed in the story of

Nicodemus—were *not born of any human stock, or by the fleshly desire of a human father* (verse 13), i.e in the ordinary way of human procreation. They were *the offspring of God himself*—brought into being by the creative power and will of God.

Then, with verse 14, comes the crowning statement: *So the Word became flesh*, i.e. a real man. God completed his long process of revelation by enclosing his saving purpose in human flesh and blood. Here is something never said before by Jew or Greek. Augustine tells us that he found all he wanted in the Greek philosophers—Plato and the rest—except this, that the Word became flesh.

Moreover, *he came to dwell among us.* So John describes Jesus' ministry, the theme of his book. The Greek verb *eskēnōsen* means literally 'pitched his tent', suggesting a temporary stay. Yet it hints at something deeper. The consonants—*s-k-n*—would remind the knowledgeable reader of the Hebrew *Shekinah*, the word the rabbis used for the Divine Presence among his people Israel. As of old God's glory had filled the tabernacle, so now it has been manifested in the person of Christ. He is 'God's presence and his very self' among men. When John says *we saw his glory*, the *we* must include the first disciples who had known Jesus in the days of his flesh. John will go on to portray the life and ministry of Jesus as 'the incarnate glory', a progressive unveiling of the splendour of God reaching its climax, by a terrific paradox, in the cross. This glory is further described as *such glory as befits the Father's only Son.* The manifested glory of the Word was the glory which the eternal Father shared with his *only* Son. This unique sonhood of Jesus, hinted at in the earlier Gospels (e.g. Matt. 11 : 27), is to be one of John's main themes. Finally, the glory is said to have been *full of grace and truth.* *Grace*, a favourite word of Paul's, is 'the extravagant goodness of God' to us undeserving men; while *truth* for John means 'eternal reality as revealed to men—either the reality itself or the revelation of it' (Dodd). *

15 Here is John's testimony to him: he cried aloud, 'This is the man I meant when I said, "He comes after me, but takes rank before me"; for before I was born, he already was.'

16 Out of his full store we have all received grace upon
17 grace; for while the Law was given through Moses, grace
18 and truth came through Jesus Christ. No one has ever seen God; but God's only Son, he who is nearest to the Father's heart, he has made him known.

✷ 15. Again the Baptist invades the Prologue to witness to Christ. Though later in time, Christ ranks before his fore-runner, for *before I [John] was born, he already was*. The words mean literally 'he was first in respect of me'. Doubtless the allusion is to Christ's pre-existence.

16 f. Out of Christ's *full store*, John says, we Christians have received *grace upon grace*—superabounding grace, wave on wave of it. The next verse explains how. The Law of the Old Testament, it says, was a real gift of God, but at best a prepara-tion for the Gospel. It set before men the Divine Command, God's moral demand upon men; but it could not do what Christ now does—give life. (The Law said, 'Do this and live'. The Gospel says, 'Live and do this'.) In Christ *grace and truth* —gracious reality—are actualized. And now, at long last, the name *Jesus Christ* appears.

18. Yet John is no mystic. Nobody, he says, has ever had direct vision of God; but in Jesus, God's only Son, his Word has (so to say) become transparent. He is 'a window into God at work'. *Nearest to the Father's heart* is the rendering of Greek that means literally 'in the bosom of the Father', an oriental phrase suggesting the *close* fellowship of a meal. Be-cause Jesus is in this intimate relation to the Father, he is able to make him known, to interpret him, to disclose his nature to men. If he has not revealed all that God is, he has revealed what it vitally concerns us to know—has revealed him as Holy Father.

In short, the story of Jesus, about to be unfolded, is the truth about God. It is the word 'God' translated into human terms and spelt out in human words and acts. All that mortal men can take in about the nature of the unseen God is ours in Jesus Christ.

N.B. Some important manuscripts here (verse 18) read *the only one, himself God*. If this reading is preferred, the sense is not affected, but Christ's deity is underlined. But the N.E.B.'s reading fits the context better. ✴

THE INTRODUCTION (I: 19–51)

✴ The Prologue over, we move to the Introduction which resumes the Baptist's witness to Jesus. One result of his testimony is that disciples attach themselves to Jesus and bear witness to him.

The paragraphs of this section are linked together by successive notes of time, so that we seem to be reading the diary of a momentous week. ✴

JOHN'S WITNESS TO ISRAEL

This is the testimony which John gave when the Jews of 19 Jerusalem sent a deputation of priests and Levites to ask him who he was. He confessed without reserve and 20 avowed, 'I am not the Messiah.' 'What then? Are you 21 Elijah?' 'No', he replied. 'Are you the prophet we await?' He answered 'No.' 'Then who are you?' they 22 asked. 'We must give an answer to those who sent us. What account do you give of yourself?' He answered in 23 the words of the prophet Isaiah: 'I am a voice crying aloud in the wilderness, "Make the Lord's highway straight."'

Some Pharisees who were in the deputation asked him, 24,25

'If you are not the Messiah, nor Elijah, nor the prophet,
26 why then are you baptizing?' 'I baptize in water,' John
replied, 'but among you, though you do not know him,
27 stands the one who is to come after me. I am not good
28 enough to unfasten his shoes.' This took place at Bethany
beyond Jordan, where John was baptizing.

* To an official Jerusalem deputation anxious about the new
religious movement, the Baptist replies that he is neither the
Messiah nor his expected forerunner (see Mal. 4: 5) nor the
prophet promised by Moses (see Deut. 18: 15) but only
Isaiah's 'voice' in the wilderness (see Isa. 40: 3). His baptism
is a preliminary rite of cleansing; but unknown among them
stands the Coming One whose slave he is not fit to be.

19. *a deputation of priests and Levites.* Higher and lower
temple officials from Jerusalem. One of their functions was to
test the claims of prophets. Hence their visit to John the
Baptist.

21. '*Are you Elijah?*' '*No*'. In Mark 9: 13 Jesus identifies
the Baptist with Elijah. This denial is puzzling if, as many
scholars hold, our evangelist knew Mark.

the prophet we await. Basing themselves on Deut. 18: 15 'The
Lord thy God will raise up unto thee a prophet...like unto
me', the Jews of Jesus' time—including the men who wrote
the Dead Sea Scrolls—looked for the coming of a new and
greater Moses in the End time. This great prophet would make
an end of all prophecy.

23. The Baptist, using Isaiah's words, declares he is but 'a
voice, a mystery', of no account beside his great Successor.

Make the Lord's highway straight. As a special road must be
cut and levelled when a king crosses the desert, so must John
prepare the way for Israel's true king.

25. *why then are you baptizing?* The Jews expected a general
purifying of God's People before the Messiah came. If John
is neither Elijah nor the Prophet, why is he plunging sinners in

Jordan? John answers in effect: 'Everything I do points away from me to my great Successor. My baptism, which is in water, is but a symbol which will soon yield to the reality [the Holy Spirit, verse 33]; for among you, unrecognized, stands the Messiah himself.' Many Jews of the time held the doctrine of a *hidden* Messiah—that Messiah was there already, incognito in Israel, waiting for the hour when God's prophet should reveal him.

27. *I am not good enough to unfasten his shoes,* i.e. not fit to be his slave. Untying his master's sandal-thong was the slave's work.

28. *Bethany beyond Jordan.* To be distinguished from Bethany near Jerusalem (11: 18). The site of Transjordan Bethany has not yet been identified. ✳

THE BAPTIST'S WITNESS TO JESUS

The next day he saw Jesus coming towards him. 'Look,' 29 he said, 'there is the Lamb of God; it is he who takes away the sin of the world. This is he of whom I spoke 30 when I said, "After me a man is coming who takes rank before me"; for before I was born, he already was. I 31 myself did not know who he was; but the very reason why I came, baptizing in water, was that he might be revealed to Israel.'

John testified further: 'I saw the Spirit coming down 32 from heaven like a dove and resting upon him. I did 33 not know him, but he who sent me to baptize in water had told me, "When you see the Spirit coming down upon someone and resting upon him you will know that this is he who is to baptize in Holy Spirit." I saw it 34 myself, and I have borne witness. This is God's Chosen One.'

✵ Some time after Jesus' Baptism (the story of which is assumed to be familiar—see verses 32 f.) the Baptist points out Jesus as *God's Chosen One*, i.e. the Messiah, declaring him to be the world's Saviour from sin and the bearer of the Holy Spirit.

Is this strict history? The Synoptic Gospels record that it was later, at Caesarea Philippi, that Peter confessed Jesus to be the Messiah. It may be then that in historical fact this recognition came only later. John is concerned to show that it did come, and that it is the truth about Jesus.

29. *The next day*. The second day of the memorable week.

the Lamb of God...who takes away the sin of the world. We naturally look to the Old Testament for a clue to these famous words. Discussion has been endless; but most probably the saying blends the idea of the Passover Lamb in Exodus 12 with the 53rd chapter of Isaiah, where the Servant of God, likened to a lamb (53: 7; cf. Acts 8: 32), is said to have borne the sin of many (53: 12). The Baptist therefore sees in Jesus a Saviour offering a new and better sacrifice for sin, a Saviour who annuls the guilt of the whole human race. Again, this is the Christian truth about Jesus, even though, in strict history, its fullness may not have been disclosed to John at Jordan.

30. *of whom I spoke*. In 1: 15.

31. *I myself did not know who he was*. John knew Jesus already, but he did not know that he was the Messiah. The purpose of his baptizing mission was to enable the hidden Messiah to be revealed. And when God revealed Messiah's identity, there stood before him Jesus of Nazareth.

32 f. John's second piece of witness to Jesus. Having seen the Spirit descend and *rest* (as an abiding possession) on Jesus, John knew by divine revelation that Jesus was the one destined to bathe men in God's Holy Spirit. In Mark it is only to Jesus himself that the vision comes: here the Baptist sees it too. Baptism with the Holy Spirit means the positive bestowal of new life, in contrast with the negative cleansing from sin implied by water-baptism.

like a dove: gently. The rabbis regarded the dove as a symbol of the Spirit.

34. Instead of *God's Chosen One* (cf. Luke 9: 35) some good MSS here read 'the Son of God'. But the meaning is not materially affected if we prefer it here. *

THE CALL OF THE DISCIPLES

The next day again John was standing with two of his 35 disciples when Jesus passed by. John looked towards him 36 and said, 'There is the Lamb of God.' The two disciples 37 heard him say this, and followed Jesus. When he turned 38 and saw them following him, he asked, 'What are you looking for?' They said, 'Rabbi' (which means a teacher), 'where are you staying?' 'Come and see', he replied. 39 So they went and saw where he was staying, and spent the rest of the day with him. It was then about four in the afternoon.

One of the two who followed Jesus after hearing what 40 John said was Andrew, Simon Peter's brother. The first 41 thing he did was to find his brother Simon. He said to him, 'We have found the Messiah' (which is the Hebrew for 'Christ'). He brought Simon to Jesus, who looked 42 him in the face, and said, 'You are Simon, son of John. You shall be called Cephas' (that is, Peter, the Rock).

The next day Jesus decided to leave for Galilee. He 43 met Philip, who, like Andrew and Peter, came from 44 Bethsaida, and said to him, 'Follow me.' Philip went to 45 find Nathanael, and told him, 'We have met the man spoken of by Moses in the Law, and by the prophets: it is Jesus son of Joseph, from Nazareth.' 'Nazareth!' 46 Nathanael exclaimed; 'can anything good come from

47 Nazareth?' Philip said, 'Come and see.' When Jesus
saw Nathanael coming, he said, 'Here is an Israelite
worthy of the name; there is nothing false in him.'
48 Nathanael asked him, 'How do you come to know me?'
Jesus replied, 'I saw you under the fig-tree before Philip
49 spoke to you.' 'Rabbi,' said Nathanael, 'you are the Son
50 of God; you are king of Israel.' Jesus answered, 'Is this
the ground of your faith, that I told you I saw you
under the fig-tree? You shall see greater things than that.'
51 Then he added, 'In truth, in very truth I tell you all,
you shall see heaven wide open, and God's angels
ascending and descending upon the Son of Man.'

✻ Compare this narrative with the call of the first disciples in
Mark 1: 16–20. Perhaps it refers to a meeting between Jesus
and his earliest disciples *before* the formal call of Mark 1: 16.
Of all the evangelists, only John records that some of Jesus'
disciples had previously followed the Baptist; but he may well
be right.

35. *The next day*. The third day of the momentous week?
One of the two disciples was Andrew—see verse 40.

39. *So they went*. They went to spend one day with Jesus
and remained to spend their lives with him.

four in the afternoon is the time when men would leave their
work. This precise record of one of life's memorable hours
suggests the memory of an eyewitness.

41. *The first thing he did was to find his brother Simon.* Shall
we call Andrew 'the first home missionary'? Some good
manuscripts read here: 'in the morning he found his brother
Simon'. This, if accepted, would give us the fourth day of the
memorable week.

We have found the Messiah. For a Jew this would be the
greatest of all discoveries.

42. *You shall be called Cephas*, i.e. 'rock man'. For Simon's

nickname see Mark 3: 16 and Matt. 16: 18. The precise occasion on which Jesus gave it to him is not certain. 'Peter' from *petra* 'rock' is the Greek equivalent of the Aramaic *Cephas*. In the Gospels Peter is not a Rock but a 'Wobbler'. Probably Jesus gave him the nickname as a prophecy (cf. Luke 22: 32) of what he would one day become. The prophecy of the name was fulfilled on the day of Pentecost—see Acts 2.

43. The fifth day? We must imagine Jesus and his men now moving up from the south into Galilee. There he encounters Philip who came *from Bethsaida* ('Fishertown') at the north end of the Lake of Galilee. Andrew and Peter were also natives of it: 'Bethsaidans'.

45. One lighted torch sets another aflame. Philip in turn finds *Nathanael* ('gift of God'). Not named in the Synoptics, he is generally identified with Bartholomew who is paired with Philip in the Synoptic lists of the disciples.

46. Nathanael's retort has become immortal. It is the scornful remark the native of one village will make of a neighbouring one. Philip's reply to it deserves a like immortality: *Come and see* is the best of all remedies for preconceived notions.

47. Jesus' praise of Nathanael is to be explained from Gen. 32: 28. There Jacob's new name was 'Israel', but he remained to the end what Esau found him—a man of guile. Nathanael, being without guile, is a better Israelite. He is willing to test the truth of the Gospel and be converted from doubt to faith.

48 f. What does Jesus mean by saying that he saw Nathanael *under the fig-tree*? The rabbis recommended men to study the Law 'under their own vine and fig-tree', i.e. at home. Nathanael is just such a Bible student, absorbed, as verse 51 suggests, in the story of Jacob's vision at Bethel.

Son of God and *king of Israel* are probably both titles of the Messiah.

51. *In truth, in very truth*, Greek *amen, amen*. The Jew *concluded* his prayers with an *Amen* (Hebrew: 'so be it', 'truly'), so expressing his faith that God would act. By contrast, Jesus

(and he alone) *prefaced* his important sayings with an *Amen*. Not only so, but, according to John, he doubled the *Amen*. Jesus thus shows that before he speaks he commits himself totally to the act of God of which his word is the channel.

The key to this important statement is to be found in Jacob's vision at Bethel (Gen. 28). But note (1) that the *Son of Man* takes the place of Jacob; and (2) that the angels go up and down on the *Son of Man* who forms a ladder between heaven and earth. Nathanael is therefore promised that in Jesus the Son of Man he will be granted a revelation of God's glory. The man Jesus is the place of revelation, the place over which the heavens are opened. In short, Nathanael and his friends are promised that they will find in the historical Jesus the one true mediator between God and men.

Nor is this all. The series of signs to follow in the Gospel, reaching a climax in the supreme sign of the cross, *is* this vision of the opened heavens. Moreover, since the Word had become flesh, these signs are *history*. Jacob's experience at Bethel might be called 'an apocalypse'—an unveiling of the glory of God. In the story about to be unfolded the disciples are promised 'a realized apocalypse'—an unveiling in history, i.e. in the life, death and resurrection of Jesus, of the glory of the eternal God. ✻

Christ the Giver of Life

THE MARRIAGE AT CANA-IN-GALILEE

2 ON THE THIRD DAY there was a wedding at Cana-in-
2 Galilee. The mother of Jesus was there, and Jesus
3 and his disciples were guests also. The wine gave out, so
4 Jesus's mother said to him, 'They have no wine left.' He
answered, 'Your concern, mother, is not mine. My

hour has not yet come.' His mother said to the servants, 5
'Do whatever he tells you.' There were six stone water- 6
jars standing near, of the kind used for Jewish rites of
purification; each held from twenty to thirty gallons.
Jesus said to the servants, 'Fill the jars with water', and 7
they filled them to the brim. 'Now draw some off', he 8
ordered, 'and take it to the steward of the feast'; and
they did so. The steward tasted the water now turned into 9
wine, not knowing its source; though the servants who
had drawn the water knew. He hailed the bridegroom
and said, 'Everyone serves the best wine first, and waits 10
until the guests have drunk freely before serving the
poorer sort; but you have kept the best wine till now.'

This deed at Cana-in-Galilee is the first of the signs by 11
which Jesus revealed his glory and led his disciples to
believe in him.

* The Introduction is over, and the first main section of the
Gospel—the revelation to the world (chs. 2–12)—is beginning.
Since at point after point it will set the New Order against the
Old, John begins with a miracle contrasting the Law and the
Gospel.

John's word for miracle is 'sign'. 'A wonder with a meaning in it' is the old definition, and John is always at pains to
bring out the 'meaning' or spiritual truth. Seven such signs he
records in the first twenty chapters; and it will be helpful to
set them down here, with their 'meanings' attached:

1. Water into wine (ch. 2)	The difference Christ makes.
2. Healing of the officer's son (ch. 4)	Faith the one thing needful.
3. Healing of the cripple (ch. 5)	Christ the restorer of lost powers.

4. Feeding of the multitude (ch. 6)   Christ the bread of life.
5. Walking on the water (ch. 6)   Christ our guide.
6. Healing of man born blind (ch. 9) Christ our light.
7. Raising of Lazarus (ch. 11)   Christ our life.

Nos. 2, 4 and 5 occur also in the Synoptics.

What are we to make of the miracle at Cana? Some simply take it literally as a creative act of God incarnate. Thus C. S. Lewis: 'Every year, as part of the Natural Order, God makes wine. He does so by creating a vegetable organism that can turn water, soil and sunlight into a juice which will, under proper conditions, become wine....Once, and in one year only, God, now incarnate, short-circuits the process: makes wine in a moment: uses earthenware jars instead of vegetable fibres to hold the water.'

Those who cannot rise to this faith in the incarnate God rationalize the miracle. Jesus (they say) bade the servants pour the water into the half-empty vessels on the table, and then by his radiant presence so gladdened the hearts of the guests that they took the diluted wine for a fresh supply of the finest vintage.

Whichever view we prefer, the historical basis must have been an actual visit of Jesus to a wedding at which somehow he saved the situation for the guests. But we shall misunderstand John if all we bother about is the 'how' of the miracle. Not the wonder, but its meaning, is his primary interest.

Even those who hold that wine in moderation has a social value realize that at a gathering where men have already 'drunk freely' the provision of a huge quantity of wine is not an act of human prudence, still less of divine compassion. This, and the position of the story at the opening of the ministry, suggest that John is here giving us a dominant theme of the Gospel. Go back to Mark 2: 19–22. There Jesus refers to himself and his disciples as a wedding party and speaks of the new wine of the kingdom of God bursting the old wine-skins of Judaism. This surely is the clue to the miracle's meaning. Jewish legalism, represented by the water of ritual purification, becomes the Gospel, the wine which gladdens the marriage-feast of the kingdom of God (Matt. 22: 1–14). Judaism is water; Christianity is wine; and it is Christ who makes all the difference. For us today the lesson is not only that we must be transformed by Christ's power, but that it must happen not in a spirit of gloomy religiosity but in the context of joyous human fellowship.

1. In the Bible *the third day* always means 'the day after tomorrow'. So here *on the third day* means 'two days after'—after the call of Nathanael (1: 43).

Cana is probably the modern Khirbet Qana eight or nine miles north of Nazareth.

4. *Your concern, mother, is not mine*. The Greek means either, 'Woman, what have you to do with me?' or 'Woman, what have you and I to do with that?' The N.E.B. favours the first, asserting the complete independence of Jesus. But the second also makes good sense: 'Never mind; don't be worried.' For 'woman' the N.E.B. has *mother*, because English has no precise equivalent for the Greek word used. 'Woman' is too cold; 'lady' too precious; 'madam' too formal.

My hour has not yet come carries a double meaning: (1) It is not time to intervene yet; and (2) It is not yet time for showing my glory.

6. *six stone water-jars*. For the guests to wash their hands in. Since each must have held about 20 gallons, their total capacity must have been over 120 gallons.

8. *the steward of the feast*. The head waiter, whose job it was to arrange the couches and taste the food and drink.

11. *Jesus revealed his glory*. We may tentatively define *glory* as 'the revelation of God's presence in saving action'. But does not this verse contradict 7: 39, 'Jesus had not yet been glorified'? The explanation is that any act of Jesus, the Word made flesh, manifests his glory, but that a *full* revelation of his glory cannot come till he has completed the work God has given him to do, i.e. until the cross. ✶

THE CLEANSING OF THE TEMPLE

12 After this he went down to Capernaum in company with his mother, his brothers, and his disciples, but they did not
13 stay there long. As it was near the time of the Jewish
14 Passover, Jesus went up to Jerusalem. There he found in the temple the dealers in cattle, sheep, and pigeons, and
15 the money-changers seated at their tables. Jesus made a whip of cords and drove them out of the temple, sheep, cattle, and all. He upset the tables of the money-changers,
16 scattering their coins. Then he turned on the dealers in pigeons: 'Take them out,' he said; 'you must not turn
17 my Father's house into a market.' His disciples recalled the words of Scripture, 'Zeal for thy house shall destroy
18 me.' The Jews challenged Jesus: 'What sign', they asked,
19 'can you show as authority for your action?' 'Destroy this temple,' Jesus replied, 'and in three days I will raise it
20 again.' They said, 'It has taken forty-six years to build this temple. Are you going to raise it again in three days?'
21, 22 But the temple he was speaking of was his body. After his resurrection his disciples recalled what he had said, and they believed the Scripture and the words that Jesus had spoken.

23 While he was in Jerusalem for Passover many gave their allegiance to him when they saw the signs that he
24 performed. But Jesus for his part would not trust himself
25 to them. He knew men so well, all of them, that he needed no evidence from others about a man, for he himself could tell what was in a man.

* After a brief stay with his family and disciples in Capernaum, Jesus moves south to Jerusalem for the approaching

Passover. There he cleanses the temple. It is a story told in all four Gospels; but John's version has its own peculiar features.

The Cleansing is far more than a Jewish reformer's act; it is a sign of the advent of the Messiah. Two Old Testament prophecies concerning 'the Day of the Lord' provide the clue to what Jesus did. One is Mal. 3: 1 ff., 'the Lord, whom ye seek, shall suddenly come to his temple... but who may abide the day of his coming... and he shall purify the sons of Levi'. The other is Zech. 14: 21, 'And there shall no longer be a trader in the house of the Lord of hosts on that day' (R.S.V.). These prophecies are now fulfilled.

Over the Old Order hangs judgement, a judgement that must begin at the house of God; and in this acted parable of judgement Jesus, condemning the Jews' impiety, proclaims that his Father's purpose in ordaining worship in his house shall be honoured and the Gentiles' right to a place in it vindicated. (Mark 11: 17, 'My house shall be called a house of prayer for all the nations'.) But John's account strongly hints that Jesus' action also signified the end of the Old Order of worship and its replacement by a new one, and that between them lay his own sacrifice and triumph which would create the New Order.

John's version of the Cleansing differs from the earlier Gospels in various ways. He alone mentions the sheep and oxen and the whip. He words Jesus' rebuke to the traders differently. He adds the quotation from Ps. 69: 9 and the saying 'Destroy this temple'. But the chief difference is that, whereas the Synoptics set the Cleansing at the beginning of Passion Week, John puts it at the beginning of Jesus' ministry. Which is likely to be historically correct? Because the Cleansing seems to belong naturally to the context of the last week when Jesus was throwing down a challenge to the religious authorities, most scholars answer: the Synoptics. John probably put it where he did for a theological reason. His purpose was to show that the judgement effected by the Messiah's presence among men operated right from the

33

beginning of the ministry. 'The Lord comes suddenly to his temple', and (as Malachi had foretold) his coming is 'like a refiner's fire'.

13. *the Jewish Passover.* This is the first of three Passovers mentioned by John—see 6: 4 and 13: 1. Like Mark, John implies that Jesus' ministry lasted over three Passovers, say, two years plus.

14 ff. Oxen, *sheep and pigeons* were needed for ritual purification before the Passover. Likewise, *money-changers* were necessary in order to turn pilgrims' foreign currency into Jewish coinage, so that they could pay the prescribed half-shekel of temple-tax.

16. Cf. Mark 11: 17 where Jesus' rebuke combines Isa. 56: 7 and Jer. 7: 11. There Jesus denounces the dishonesty of the traders. Here it is the trade itself which is condemned. Note the *my Father* (not 'our Father' or 'your Father') with its suggestion of unique Sonhood, and compare the 'my Father's house' of the boy Jesus (Luke 2: 49).

17. Ps. 69: 9. As the psalmist suffered for his *zeal* for God's *house*, so Christ's Cleansing of the Temple will *destroy* him.

18. The Jews' challenge here is like that in Mark 11: 28.

19. Jesus' answer to the Jews' demand for a sign. This is doubtless the saying which was quoted—in a garbled version—against Jesus at his trial (Mark 14: 58; cf. Acts 6: 14).

Destroy is a 'prophetic' command meaning, 'Go on as you are doing and you will bring this temple down in ruin (at the hands of Rome) but in a brief time (three days) I will raise up another centre of worship'. Jesus is predicting that through his work there will arise a new spiritual building in which the New Israel, the Church, will worship God.

20. The Jews take the saying quite literally as a claim that he will do in three days' time what labourers had been working for nearly half a century to complete.

forty-six years. An historical note with the ring of truth. Herod the Great began the rebuilding of the Temple in 20–19 B.C. This dates the Cleansing to A.D. 27 or 28.

21. The evangelist's comment. Jesus (he says) was referring to his human body as the shrine of God's presence—of the incarnate Word. But there may be also an allusion to Christ's *mystical* Body, for as a result of the resurrection there arose what Paul calls 'the Body of Christ', the new community of which Christ is the living head, the Church.

22. *the Scripture.* Possibly a reference to Ps. 16: 10.

23 f. These verses describe Jesus' sojourn *in Jerusalem* and the believers won over by his signs. But, comments John, Jesus set no store by this miracle-made faith (Luther called it 'milk faith') because he was too shrewd a reader of human nature to be unduly impressed by it. *

NICODEMUS

There was one of the Pharisees named Nicodemus, a **3** member of the Jewish Council, who came to Jesus by 2 night. 'Rabbi,' he said, 'we know that you are a teacher sent by God; no one could perform these signs of yours unless God were with him.' Jesus answered, 'In truth, 3 in very truth I tell you, unless a man has been born over again he cannot see the kingdom of God.' 'But how is it 4 possible', said Nicodemus, 'for a man to be born when he is old? Can he enter his mother's womb a second time and be born?' Jesus answered, 'In truth I tell you, no 5 one can enter the kingdom of God without being born from water and spirit. Flesh can give birth only to flesh; 6 it is spirit that gives birth to spirit. You ought not to be 7 astonished, then, when I tell you that you must be born over again. The wind blows where it wills; you hear the 8 sound of it, but you do not know where it comes from, or where it is going. So with everyone who is born from spirit.'

9, 10   Nicodemus replied, 'How is this possible?' 'What!'
said Jesus. 'Is this famous teacher of Israel ignorant of
11   such things? In very truth I tell you, we speak of what
we know, and testify to what we have seen, and yet you
12   all reject our testimony. If you disbelieve me when I
talk to you about things on earth, how are you to believe
if I should talk about the things of heaven?

13   'No one ever went up into heaven except the one who
came down from heaven, the Son of Man whose home is
14   in heaven. This Son of Man must be lifted up as the
15   serpent was lifted up by Moses in the wilderness, so that
everyone who has faith in him may in him possess eternal
life.

✳ Quite abruptly, and in the context of his stay in Jerusalem,
we learn of Jesus' encounter by night with Nicodemus, a
member of the Sanhedrin, the supreme Jewish religious court.
    Note that by means of these encounters (Nicodemus, the
Samaritan woman, etc.) John is able to depict the inbreaking
of the New Age and Jesus as the Messiah. (The New Order,
however, does not arrive without fierce opposition from the
Jews: therefore John also gives us glimpses of the struggle
between the old and the new which climaxed in the cross.)
Note also that the dialogue here, beginning from the idea of
rebirth, branches out into discourse about the whole work of
Christ.
    Nicodemus, one of Israel's theologians, comes to Jesus under
cover of darkness to learn more about the new movement. He
begins with compliments—sincere enough, so far as they go.
But Jesus meets his diplomatic approaches by asserting the
need for a completely new start. What is wanted in face of
God's New Order is not more information, but such a re-
orientation as can only be compared to new birth. (The
rabbis of the time, we are told, had no real doctrine of

regeneration, as spiritual rebirth is called.) 'Impossible!' replies
Nicodemus, thinking Jesus is talking about physical rebirth.
But Jesus' mind is on spiritual regeneration. Like a good Jew,
Nicodemus is waiting for the kingdom of God. Then let him
know that God only can work the spiritual miracle needed for
entry into the kingdom.

Jesus' theme, then, is the need for repentance—for a complete 'right-about-turn'. But what does he mean by the need
to be reborn of *water and spirit*? Nicodemus could not plead
that he did not know what *born of water* meant—everybody in
Israel had heard of John's water-baptism. But (says Jesus) a
candidate for God's kingdom (or New Order) needs also to
be bathed in the Holy Spirit, which is the gift of John's
successor. In short, Jesus is saying to Nicodemus: 'Do what
my disciples have done: first, submit to John's baptism, and
then come, join my company in whom the power of the New
Order is working.'

Then, as they talk, the night wind rustles round their place
of meeting. It offers a vivid analogy. 'The wind blows as it
wills,' says Jesus, 'where it comes from and where it goes is a
mystery. Yet how real and powerful a thing it is! So is God's
wind, the Spirit, and so incontestable is its effect on a man's
life.' In other words, the workings of God's Spirit, like the
wind's movements, cannot be traced. Yet it offers Nicodemus
the thing he desperately needs. Let him avail himself of it
now. (Is not such regeneration the only real cure still for 'our
human predicament'?)

But Nicodemus, rapidly being swept out of his depth, remains incredulous. 'Is this all news to you, one of the Church's
recognized theologians?' Jesus asks him. 'Why, with us [i.e.
Jesus and his disciples] this is matter of familiar experience.
Though you leaders in Israel deny them, we know that such
spiritual miracles happen. I have used natural illustrations—
wind, water, birth. But if such earthly analogies mean nothing to you, how can you expect to follow me when I speak of
divine mysteries' (e.g. the love of God)?

Life moves at two levels, flesh and spirit—human and divine, with a gulf between them. That gulf can only be spanned from above. But it has been spanned by the Son of Man (here Jesus speaks in veiled terms of himself). He alone has experience of the heavenly world, and he must be lifted up, like the wilderness serpent, in order that those who look trustingly on him may live—eternally.

As John sets down these words, which hint at the coming cross, he knows that his Christian readers will take the point, will understand that the place of death is the place of revelation, and the source of the new life which is the Gospel's gift.

1. *Nicodemus* (a Greek name), not mentioned in the Synoptics, appears thrice in this Gospel: here, at 7: 50 and at 19: 39.

3. *born over again.* The Greek means both 'from above' and 'over again'. Probably both are meant here, since the rebirth is certainly from above. The Synoptic parallel is Matt. 18: 3.

5. *no one can enter the kingdom of God without being born from water and spirit.* The meaning must be the same as in verse 3, *born over again.* Birth from the spirit is equivalent to birth from above (or birth over again). The phrasing suggests Christian baptism. Before we convict John of anachronism, we should consider Ezek. 36: 25 ff., where God promises to cleanse his people with 'clean water' and 'a new spirit'.

8. *The wind blows where it wills.* There is a play on words here. The Greek word means both 'wind' and 'spirit'. Either of these translations, taken by itself, would be wrong. John meant both, but in English we cannot represent his double meaning.

12. *things on earth.* Water, wind and birth, used as analogies. *things of heaven.* The divine mysteries of God's love and eternal life.

13. *whose home is in heaven.* These words, omitted by some good MSS, may well belong to the true text, as the N.E.B. assumes. They are true to John's thought, which is that Christ does not cease to be with the Father—and so in heaven—even while he walks the ways of earth.

14. The Old Testament reference is to Num. 21: 9. The point of the simile is that the brazen serpent was raised up so that all could see it, and all who looked at it lived. So *this Son of Man must be lifted up*. The Greek means (1) lift up (on a cross), and (2) exalt (to heaven). It has both meanings here, for John teaches that the cross is the beginning of Jesus' ascent to the Father. The verb therefore at once raises our minds to Calvary and to the heavenly throne. Note the word *must*. It is the 'must' of divine necessity. God's will points this way. Cf. Mark 8: 31.

15. *eternal life*. The central concept of this Gospel, occurring 17 times in it (and 6 times in 1 John). It stands for the salvation described in the Synoptics as entrance into the kingdom of God—a phrase found in John only in verses 3 and 5 of this chapter. (But study Mark 10: 17–31 and you will find that to follow Jesus = to inherit eternal life = to enter the kingdom of God = to be saved.) Eternal life is to be distinguished from 'everlasting life'—a mere going on and on. It is a qualitative term, denoting the life which is life indeed, life lived in communion with God through Christ, life with the quality of eternity about it, life that therefore can never die.

Though its fullness belongs to the heavenly world, John teaches that it is a blessing which believers foretaste here and now:

'To have part in the divine life of Jesus Christ by faith, to stand in the midst of history and be comprehended in eternal salvation, through the reconciliation made in Him who is called the Life and the Way to Life—this is to be a Christian—to have life eternal' (Brunner). ✷

SALVATION AND JUDGEMENT

'God loved the world so much that he gave his only 16 Son, that everyone who has faith in him may not die but have eternal life. It was not to judge the world that God 17 sent his Son into the world, but that through him the world might be saved.

18 'The man who puts his faith in him does not come under judgement; but the unbeliever has already been judged in that he has not given his allegiance to God's 19 only Son. Here lies the test: the light has come into the world, but men preferred darkness to light because their 20 deeds were evil. Bad men all hate the light and avoid 21 it, for fear their practices should be shown up. The honest man comes to the light so that it may be clearly seen that God is in all he does.'

✳ These verses are the evangelist's soliloquy (note the *past* tenses employed) rather than words of Jesus (as the N.E.B. assumes—witness its inverted commas).

John does not tell us whether Nicodemus believed or disbelieved any more than, later, he will tell us what the Samaritan woman did. This does not mean that Nicodemus and the woman are only symbols. John's overriding concern is to draw out the deepest meaning of what Christ's coming means to men. This he now does.

Verse 13 had spoken of the descent of the Son of Man. This means, in Christian terms, the Incarnation and the Atonement. And these, John says, have their origin in the love of God. *God loved the world so much that he gave his only Son.* This verse Luther called 'the Gospel within the Gospels'. Sometimes we sum up the message of Christianity as 'God is love'. But the Gospel is more than an idea, however sublime. It is a once-for-all *act* of God in human history. God *gave*: gave has the double sense of 'sent' and 'delivered up to die'. It was an act infinitely costly to God—'He did not spare his own Son, but surrendered him for us all' says Paul (Rom. 8: 32), echoing the story of Abraham and his son. And it was an act which concerned not a handful of believers but the whole world of men. What was its purpose? *That everyone who has faith in him*

40

may not die but have eternal life. The condition is *faith*, i.e. personal trust. The blessing is *eternal life*. And the alternative is death—not merely the death of the body but final separation from God the fountain of life.

God's primary purpose, then, in sending his Son, was salvation, not judgement (verse 17). Did not Jesus himself say that the Son of Man was come to seek and to save that which was lost (Luke 19: 10)? Yet, as John goes on to say, judgement, i.e. sifting and discrimination, there must always be where Christ is. And so in verses 18–21 he sets forth the consequences of faith and unbelief in the incarnate Son of God. Just as Paul says that 'there is no condemnation for those who are united with Christ' (Rom. 8: 1), so John declares that the man who personally trusts Christ is lifted out of the realm of God's judgement. But there is another and dark side to the medal. Face to face with Christ, we cannot be neutrals, balanced between belief and unbelief; and so, *the unbeliever has already been judged in that he has not given his allegiance to God's only Son.* If a man refuses to trust in the Son of God, no further verdict is needed, for his own conduct finds him guilty. For John, Doomsday is not primarily a far-off end-of-the-world event, but a present process. Though Christ did not come to 'judge' the world, i.e. pass sentence on it, men judge themselves by the attitude they take up to him. John had Jesus' authority for this: 'Whoever then will acknowledge me before men, I will acknowledge him before my Father in heaven; and whoever disowns me before men, I will disown him before my Father in heaven' (Matt. 10: 32 f.). To refuse Christ then is to sentence oneself. Somebody has said that the primary purpose of the sun is not to cast shadows, but it does. So it is with him who is the light of the world.

Verses 19–21 expound this doctrine of judgement in strongly ethical terms. *Here lies the test* is the N.E.B.'s rendering of 'This is the judgement', and the picture is of bad men hurrying away from the radiance of a central light, conscious that their evil deeds cannot stand its searching beam.

41

Bad men, John says, *all hate the light and avoid it, for fear their practices should be shown up. The honest man*, by contrast, *comes to the light so that it may be clearly seen that God is in all he does*. The N.E.B.'s *honest man* is, literally, 'he that does the truth'. Truth is something to be *done*, not merely believed, and 'a right act is so much of the truth made visible'. ✻

THE FINAL WITNESS OF THE BAPTIST TO JESUS

22 After this, Jesus went into Judaea with his disciples, stayed
23 there with them, and baptized. John too was baptizing at Aenon, near to Salim, because water was plentiful in that region; and people were constantly coming for
24 baptism. This was before John's imprisonment.

25 Some of John's disciples had fallen into a dispute with
26 Jews about purification; so they came to him and said, 'Rabbi, there was a man with you on the other side of the Jordan, to whom you bore your witness. Here he is,
27 baptizing, and crowds are flocking to him.' John's answer
28 was: 'A man can have only what God gives him. You yourselves can testify that I said, "I am not the Messiah; I
29 have been sent as his forerunner." It is the bridegroom to whom the bride belongs. The bridegroom's friend, who stands by and listens to him, is overjoyed at hearing the bridegroom's voice. This joy, this perfect joy, is now
30 mine. As he grows greater, I must grow less.'

✻ The earlier evangelists are silent about this concurrent ministry of Jesus and John; but there is nothing historically improbable about it.

In the earlier Gospels Jesus, after declaring the Baptist to be the greatest born of woman, yet places him outside the kingdom of God (Matt. 11:11; Luke 7:28). So here the Baptist is a representative of the Old Order, but the supreme one, because he brings the bride (Israel) to the bridegroom (Christ). (Cf. Mark 2: 19 for the metaphor.) And having seen the daughter of Israel pass to her proper husband, the Baptist rejoices in 'his harsh, negative mission', and withdraws to prison and death.

22. *Judaea.* The neighbourhood of Jordan. Only here, verse 26, and 4: 1 are we told in the Gospels that Jesus baptized; and in 4: 2 it is made clear that Jesus left the actual performance of the rite to the disciples.

23. *Aenon, near to Salim* is east of Mt Gerizim and Nablus (Shechem). Nearby is the modern *Ainun* ('little fountain') and many springs.

24. *This was before John's imprisonment.* Cf. Mark 1: 14, 'After John had been arrested, Jesus came into Galilee'. Everything so far related preceded the Galilean ministry of which the Synoptics tell.

25. The occasion for John's final testimony was a dispute between *Jews* (some good MSS read 'a Jew') and John's disciples about purification. Was it about the efficacy of Jesus' baptism compared with John's?

26 f. When his disciples tell the Baptist, he makes a noble reply. Such success as Jesus is winning can only be God-given. He himself had never claimed to be the Messiah, only his fore-runner. The bridegroom (the Messiah) has now appeared, and the forerunner sincerely rejoices in his success.

29. John calls himself 'the best man', whereas Jesus is the bridegroom. The bride, as often in the Old Testament, is Israel. It was the 'best man's' duty to bring bride and bride-groom together; and John, having presented the bride to her groom, withdraws. His joy is complete, because he has finished the work God gave him to do. ✶

COMMENT BY THE EVANGELIST

He who comes from above is above all others; he who is ³¹ from the earth belongs to the earth and uses earthly speech. He who comes from heaven bears witness to what he ³²

33 has seen and heard, yet no one accepts his witness. To
34 accept his witness is to attest that God speaks true; for he
whom God sent utters the words of God, so measureless
35 is God's gift of the Spirit. The Father loves the Son and
36 has entrusted him with all authority. He who puts his
faith in the Son has hold of eternal life, but he who
disobeys the Son shall not see that life; God's wrath rests
upon him.

✶ The evangelist adds a comment contrasting Jesus with his
forerunner. He describes Christ as God's ambassador to men,
and declares the consequences of belief or unbelief in him.

31. The one *from above* is Christ; the one *from the earth*,
the Baptist. But John was 'earthly' only in the sense that
his mission was to prepare the way on earth for the Man from
heaven.

32 ff. The Baptist's inspiration is not denied; but in an
earthly prophet like John inspiration comes and goes; whereas
God gives his Spirit 'measurelessly' to Christ as his beloved
Son.

35. John's equivalent of Matt. 11: 27.

36. John faces his readers with the decisive either-or,
belief or unbelief. True belief in God's Son (life-trust, not lip-
credence) does not earn eternal life; it is it. But he who rejects
the Son not only deprives himself of that life, but incurs God's
abiding displeasure. *God's wrath*, mentioned only here in the
Gospel, occurs commonly in Paul. Nowadays, sentimentally
minded Christians would like to forget that the Bible uses
such 'horrid' language about God. Yet wrath is part of any
true conception of God as a moral being to whom sin is hate-
ful; and if we believe that 'world history is world judgement',
there is plenty of evidence for it in the world today. Such
wrath is not 'the outbursting of irritated pride', as it tends to
be in human beings. To form a true picture of it, we should
think of the holy indignation which a good man feels in the

presence of stark evil (like Lincoln's when he saw a slave-market for the first time)—and then multiply it infinitely. Such wrath must belong to him whose nature is Holy Love. ✳

THE WOMAN OF SAMARIA

✳ The story of the woman of Samaria is one of the most life-like in the Gospel. Behind it, even if the evangelist may have shaped it for his purpose, must lie real history. (Luke 9: 51-6 and 17: 11-19 supply independent evidence of Jesus' activity in Samaria.)

Apparently to avoid growing opposition, Jesus leaves Judaea for Galilee and passes en route through Samaria. At Jacob's well—and in the East all sorts of interesting things happen at wells—he meets a Samaritan woman. Out of a simple request for a drink there grows a conversation which culminates in the disclosure of his Messiahship.

On the theological level, we should note that both at the beginning and the end of Christ's conversation with the woman there is a contrast between the Old Order and the New. First, water from Jacob's well is not to be compared with the water which Jesus gives. Second, both the Jewish worship at Jerusalem and the Samaritan on Gerizim are to be replaced by a truly catholic worship.

We shall break up the story into three parts. ✳

JACOB'S WELL AND THE WATER OF LIFE

A report now reached the Pharisees: 'Jesus is winning and **4** baptizing more disciples than John'; although, in fact, it 2 was only the disciples who were baptizing and not Jesus himself. When Jesus learned this, he left Judaea and set out 3 once more for Galilee. He had to pass through Samaria, 4 and on his way came to a Samaritan town called Sychar, 5 near the plot of ground which Jacob gave to his son

6 Joseph and the spring called Jacob's well. It was about noon, and Jesus, tired after his journey, sat down by the well.

8 The disciples had gone away to the town to buy food.
7 Meanwhile a Samaritan woman came to draw water.
9 Jesus said to her, 'Give me a drink.' The Samaritan woman said, 'What! You, a Jew, ask a drink of me, a Samaritan woman?' (Jews and Samaritans, it should be
10 noted, do not use vessels in common.) Jesus answered her, 'If only you knew what God gives, and who it is that is asking you for a drink, you would have asked him and he
11 would have given you living water.' 'Sir,' the woman said, 'you have no bucket and this well is deep. How can
12 you give me "living water"? Are you a greater man than Jacob our ancestor, who gave us the well, and drank from it himself, he and his sons, and his cattle too?'
13 Jesus said, 'Everyone who drinks this water will be thirsty
14 again, but whoever drinks the water that I shall give him will never suffer thirst any more. The water that I shall give him will be an inner spring always welling up for eternal
15 life.' 'Sir,' said the woman, 'give me that water, and then I shall not be thirsty, nor have to come all this way to draw.'

✻ 1 ff. The Pharisees' jealousy of Jesus' success seems to have caused his departure. With verse 2 compare 3: 22, 26. Why this correction? Jesus sanctioned baptism but left the actual performance of it to his disciples. We can understand why Jesus' disciples later regarded it as necessary (Acts 2: 38) if before the crucifixion they had practised it with his authority.

4 f. *He had to pass through Samaria.* This was the quicker route from Judaea to Galilee; but, to avoid inhospitable Samaria, pilgrims often took the route by Peraea. *Sychar* has

46

been commonly identified with the modern *Askar* at the foot
of Mt Ebal, half a mile from Jacob's well which still exists (see
map on p. ix).

6. *tired after his journey*. Though no evangelist more clearly
depicts Jesus' divinity, John also makes it clear that he was bone
of our bone, flesh of our flesh.

7–10. The disciples' absence may explain Jesus' request to
the woman. They would have met his need, but perhaps they
had gone off taking the rope and the skin-bucket with them.
What! You, a Jew, ask a drink of me, a Samaritan woman? Two
excellent reasons for her surprise: (1) She was a woman, and
the rabbis laid it down that 'a man should not salute a woman
in a public place', even if she were his wife; and (2) she was a
Samaritan sectarian. The note in 9*b* is the evangelist's explanation. Jews did not *use vessels in common* with Samaritans for
fear of incurring ritual uncleanness. Then Jesus tries to find a
point of contact with the woman whereby he may meet her
spiritual need. If only she had known her questioner (he says),
she would have been asking the favour and would have got
living water. 'Living water' suggests the flowing water of a
stream as opposed to the static water of a well; but Jesus'
phrase deliberately hints at something deeper—at the water of
life.

11–15. 'Living water?' rejoins the woman, 'but you have
no bucket to draw it with.' Besides, her Samaritan pride rises
up at the idea that a Jew could produce running water where
the patriarch Jacob had been forced to sink a deep well. Does
the stranger imagine he is greater than the patriarch? Yes,
Jesus replies, his gift (the water of life) is greater, being
inexhaustible. It is the reality of which Jacob's water is but a
symbol. It is a spring welling up permanently within a man,
making him a new creature. It is the water of eternal life. But
the woman does not yet quite understand Jesus. 'Give me this
new water of yours,' she says, 'and save me all this drudgery
of drawing.' But Jesus is leading her on to deeper things. ✳

THE TRUE WORSHIP OF GOD

16 Jesus replied, 'Go home, call your husband and come
17 back.' She answered, 'I have no husband.' 'You are
right', said Jesus, 'in saying that you have no husband,
18 for, although you have had five husbands, the man with
whom you are now living is not your husband; you told
19 me the truth there.' 'Sir,' she replied, 'I can see that you
20 are a prophet. Our fathers worshipped on this mountain,
but you Jews say that the temple where God should be
21 worshipped is in Jerusalem.' 'Believe me,' said Jesus, 'the
time is coming when you will worship the Father neither
22 on this mountain, nor in Jerusalem. You Samaritans
worship without knowing what you worship, while we
worship what we know. It is from the Jews that salvation
23 comes. But the time approaches, indeed it is already here,
when those who are real worshippers will worship the
Father in spirit and in truth. Such are the worshippers
24 whom the Father wants. God is spirit, and those who
25 worship him must worship in spirit and in truth.' The
woman answered, 'I know that Messiah' (that is Christ)
'is coming. When he comes he will tell us everything.'
26 Jesus said, 'I am he, I who am speaking to you now.'

✻ 16. *call your husband.* The moment of truth. Seeking to
arouse her sense of need through her sense of guilt, Jesus elicits
a confession from the woman: *I have no husband.* Jesus agrees:
her present husband is not really her husband but her lover,
and her previous number of husbands is no credit to her.
(Jewish opinion regarded three as the absolute limit.) This
thought-reading and exposure of her sin leads her to pronounce him a seer able to unveil the guilty secrets of her past.
So (verse 19) she changes the subject, asking now for a ruling

on the ancient dispute between Jew and Samaritan: Mt Zion
or Mt Gerizim—which is the true place of worship? (After
the Return from the Exile the Jews had excluded the Samaritans from the temple on Mt Zion, and the latter had set up a
rival shrine on Mt Gerizim.) Jesus' reply leads the discussion
to where that issue does not arise at all. The day for such local
rivalries, he says, is over. The Samaritans worship what is in
effect an unknown God: Israel alone is the school of the true
knowledge of God. But all this is to be changed—indeed the
new era is beginning now—an era in which local religious
rivalries will yield to a universal worship of the Father, a
worship that will be spiritual, inward, real. With a faint ink-
ling of his meaning but still unable to discern in the stranger
the Word made flesh, she continues the dialogue: 'Yes,' she
says, 'Messiah is coming. He will settle all our disputes. We
must wait for him.' To which comes the tremendous rejoinder:
'He is here now—talking to you.'

20. *this mountain.* Gerizim.

22. The Samaritans accepted Yahweh (or Jehovah, as the
name is often spelt) as the true God, but knew little about him.
Holding only the first five books of the Old Testament to be
inspired scripture, they denied themselves the revelation given
through prophet and psalmist.

It is from the Jews that salvation comes. Or, as Athanasius put
it, 'the commonwealth of Israel was the school of the knowledge of God for all nations'.

23. *it is already here.* God's New Order is no longer a
shining hope on the far horizon; it is a present reality. (In the
Synoptics Jesus' words often strike the same note—see, for
example, Matt. 13: 16 f.; Luke 10: 23 f.) In Jesus' words and
works, fully endowed as he is with the Spirit, that is already
realized which will come to his followers when, his work
completed, they receive the Spirit which was his.

24. *God is spirit.* Not, as the A.V. says, 'God is a spirit'.
What is stressed is the essential being, not the personality, of
God. And when we think of God as spirit, we should think

'not of an infinite spiritual essence in repose but of an infinite spiritual power in action' (Forsyth).

25. The Samaritans also cherished the hope of a Messiah, their name for him being Restorer. ✳

HARVEST IN SAMARIA

27 At that moment his disciples returned, and were astonished to find him talking with a woman; but none of them said, 'What do you want?' or, 'Why are you talking
28 with her?' The woman put down her water-jar and went
29 away to the town, where she said to the people, 'Come and see a man who has told me everything I ever did.
30 Could this be the Messiah?' They came out of the town and made their way towards him.

31 Meanwhile the disciples were urging him, 'Rabbi, have
32 something to eat.' But he said, 'I have food to eat of
33 which you know nothing.' At this the disciples said to one another, 'Can someone have brought him food?'
34 But Jesus said, 'It is meat and drink for me to do the will of him who sent me until I have finished his work.

35 'Do you not say, "Four months more and then comes harvest"? But look, I tell you, look round on the fields;
36 they are already white, ripe for harvest. The reaper is drawing his pay and gathering a crop for eternal life, so
37 that sower and reaper may rejoice together. That is how the saying comes true: "One sows, and another reaps."
38 I sent you to reap a crop for which you have not toiled. Others toiled and you have come in for the harvest of their toil.'

39 Many Samaritans of that town came to believe in him because of the woman's testimony: 'He told me every-

thing I ever did.' So when these Samaritans had come to 40
him they pressed him to stay with them; and he stayed
there two days. Many more became believers because of 41
what they heard from his own lips. They told the woman, 42
'It is no longer because of what you said that we believe,
for we have heard him ourselves; and we know that this is
in truth the Saviour of the world.'

✻ The excited woman, leaving her water-jar, goes off to the
town with the news that she may have found the Messiah;
while the disciples, returning with food, invite Jesus to eat,
only to be told that another kind of food—the doing of God's
will—is his concern. Then the disciples, glancing at the sown
fields, observe, 'It will be harvest-tide in four months' time'.
But Jesus, noting the Samaritans approaching, says, 'The harvest is now here—ready for the reapers'. It is a harvest on
which other labourers (he means the Baptist and his disciples)
have long toiled: and they, the disciples, are now called to
reap the crop. The woman's testimony persuades some to
believe in Christ, but still more are convinced by hearing him
for themselves. Yet, in spite of his success, he stays only two
days among them: his true work was among the Jews.

The heart of this passage is the parable in verses 35–38. To
understand it, remember not only that the prophets had
likened 'the day of the Lord' to harvest-time but that in the
Synoptics Jesus had compared the coming of God's reign in
his own mission to the harvest and had declared it to be under
way (see Matt. 9: 37 f.; Luke 10: 2). The equivalent of the
Synoptic 'The harvest truly is plentiful' is here: *look round on
the fields; they are already white, ripe for harvest.*

28. *The woman put down her water-jar.* She meant to come
back and was in a great hurry. A little bit of realism; attempts
to find a symbolical meaning here are misplaced.

34. A complete description of Jesus' mission (cf. 5: 36 and
17: 4).

35. Not a rural proverb, as some have said. With the material harvest Jesus contrasts the spiritual. In the latter the process has been telescoped and the harvest is here. Acts 8: 5–25 records how later Philip the evangelist and, after him, Peter and John were to gather in many sheaves.

37. This may have been originally a rural proverb. Jesus applies it to the situation before him. The reaper has overtaken the sower: the harvest is here: it is the time of fulfilment.

38. *Others toiled.* Jesus refers to the work of the Baptist and his followers at *Aenon, near to Salim* (3: 23) which had made the Samaritan people receptive to his message.

39 f. The Samaritan 'dissenters' invite Jesus to stay with them, while the Jerusalem Jews drive him away.

41 f. Note the contrast between faith based on what others tell us and faith founded on personal experience. The latter is of course of prime importance; but the Bible finds a place for the other kind too: cf. Ps. 44: 1,

> our fathers have told us,
> What work thou didst in their days,
> in the days of old. ✳

THE OFFICER'S SON

43, 44 When the two days were over he set out for Galilee; for Jesus himself declared that a prophet is without honour in
45 his own country. On his arrival in Galilee the Galileans gave him a welcome, because they had seen all that he did at the festival in Jerusalem; they had been at the festival themselves.

46 Once again he visited Cana-in-Galilee, where he had turned the water into wine. An officer in the royal service
47 was there, whose son was lying ill at Capernaum. When he heard that Jesus had come from Judaea into Galilee, he came to him and begged him to go down and cure his

son, who was at the point of death. Jesus said to him, 48
'Will none of you ever believe without seeing signs and
portents?' The officer pleaded with him, 'Sir, come down 49
before my boy dies.' Then Jesus said, 'Return home; your 50
son will live.' The man believed what Jesus said and
started for home. When he was on his way down his 51
servants met him with the news, 'Your boy is going to
live.' So he asked them what time it was when he got 52
better. They said, 'Yesterday at one in the afternoon the
fever left him.' The father noted that this was the exact 53
time when Jesus had said to him, 'Your son will live', and
he and all his household became believers.

This was now the second sign which Jesus performed 54
after coming down from Judaea into Galilee.

* Verses 43-5 supply a short itinerary leading up to the story
of the officer's son.

This is another version of the story we know from the
Synoptics as the Centurion's Servant (Matt. 8: 5-13; Luke 7:
10). (The variation between 'servant' and 'son' springs from
the ambiguity of the Greek word neatly translated 'boy' in
the N.E.B.—which could mean both.) The outline of the
story in both traditions—the soldier's appeal, the healing at a
distance, the recovery at the very same hour, the dominant
theme of faith—is so similar as to rule out any other conclusion.
On the other hand, the differences in detail—and in dialogue
—between John and the Synoptics strongly suggest that John
drew the story from an independent tradition.

As with the Syro-Phoenician woman's daughter (Mark 7:
24-30) Jesus' miracle here was wrought at a distance. Some
try to explain what happened in non-miraculous terms. Jesus,
they suggest, having learned the boy's symptoms from his
father, confidently predicted his recovery, and his prognosis
(as our doctors would say) was hailed as superhuman. We

prefer to believe that its secret is to be sought in the person of Jesus and his power of prayer. 'I think,' wrote David S. Cairns, 'the Gospel view of miracles is quite plainly that they are the works of his own faith in God, and of the Divine Spirit in answer to the appeal of his faith. They are answers to his prayers; and it is my faith that if we could pray like him, we should see like issues.'

The point of the story for us today is: faith the one thing needful. What is needed in us is a faith which refuses to take No for an answer—faith that the living and reigning Christ can meet our needs.

44. Cf. Mark 6: 4. Here Judaea seems to be Jesus' *own country*, not Galilee, as we should have expected. This is probably what John meant. Judaea was his 'own home' where 'his own people' did not receive him. Jerusalem, not Galilee, is the place where Messiah must work and die.

46. *An officer in the royal service*. Literally, 'a king's man' (cf. 'centurion' in the Synoptics). This man—a non-Jew, according to Matthew and Luke—was in the army of Herod Antipas, tetrarch of Galilee, commonly but inaccurately called 'king'.

48. *Will none of you ever believe without seeing signs and portents?* Note the plural. The officer had faith, but not the surrounding Galileans whom Jesus had known from his boyhood. They would believe only if they had something quite spectacular to convince them.

54. *This was now the second sign.* The first was at Cana. Since it tells how Christ's word gave life to one as good as dead, it is a sign of the life-giving Word; for 'Christ was the Word and spake it'. ✳

CURE OF A CRIPPLE ON THE SABBATH

5 Later on Jesus went up to Jerusalem for one of the Jewish
2 festivals. Now at the Sheep-Pool in Jerusalem there is a place with five colonnades. Its name in the language of

the Jews is Bethesda. In these colonnades there lay a ₃
crowd of sick people, blind, lame, and paralysed. Among ₅
them was a man who had been crippled for thirty-eight
years. When Jesus saw him lying there and was aware ₆
that he had been ill a long time, he asked him, 'Do you
want to recover?' 'Sir,' he replied, 'I have no one to put ₇
me in the pool when the water is disturbed, but while I
am moving, someone else is in the pool before me.' Jesus ₈
answered, 'Rise to your feet, take up your bed and walk.'
The man recovered instantly, took up his stretcher, and ₉
began to walk.

That day was a Sabbath. So the Jews said to the man ₁₀
who had been cured, 'It is the Sabbath. You are not
allowed to carry your bed on the Sabbath.' He answered, ₁₁
'The man who cured me said, "Take up your bed and
walk."' They asked him, 'Who is the man who told you ₁₂
to take up your bed and walk?' But the cripple who had ₁₃
been cured did not know; for the place was crowded and
Jesus had slipped away. A little later Jesus found him in ₁₄
the temple and said to him, 'Now that you are well again,
leave your sinful ways, or you may suffer something
worse.' The man went away and told the Jews that it was ₁₅
Jesus who had cured him.

✻ This story of a cripple's cure at the Pool of Bethesda tells
how Jesus clashed with the religious authorities in Jerusalem.
It is the first episode in a growing conflict between faith and
unbelief.

Why did John choose to relate this particular miracle?
Possibly because it involved his favourite symbol of water.
The water of the Pool, though it seemed to offer healing
(or newness of life), had yet failed to cure a man crippled
for thirty-eight years. In the light of the Prologue and the

preceding chapters (the water and wine of Cana, the new water which Jesus offered the woman of Samaria) we are perhaps meant to think of 'the law given through Moses' and its failure to give life. Over against it, in this miracle, stands the life-giving word of Christ.

But we should also see in the story a sign of the truth declared in Mark 2: 28 that 'the Son of Man is sovereign even over the Sabbath'. The rabbis had taught the Jews to see in the Sabbath commanded in the Law a kind of ritual foretaste of the true Sabbath, i.e. the Messianic Age. The Law sabbath was the shadow; the Messianic Age, when it came, was to be the reality (see Heb. 4: 1–10). The reason why his enemies were so angered at Jesus' attitude to the Sabbath (he seemed to go out of his way to heal on the hallowed day) is that his actions involved the claim to be the Messiah and therefore Lord of the Sabbath. If he heals on the Sabbath, it is because the Messianic Age has dawned.

1. *one of the Jewish festivals.* Presumably a minor one, as distinct from 'the big three'—Passover, Pentecost and Tabernacles.

2. *the Sheep-Pool in Jerusalem...Bethesda.* In 1931–2 excavators laid bare 100 yards north of the Temple what is almost certainly the long-lost Pool of Bethesda.

3 f. Our translators have left out verses 3 *b* and 4 with their reference to the angel that went down into the pool and troubled the waters (see 5: 4 in the A.V.). They have done so because its omission by our best manuscripts plus its 'un-Johannine' language show it to be something a scribe inserted into the text, no doubt to explain the troubling of the waters in verse 7.

8. *Rise to your feet, take up your bed and walk.* Almost the same words as Jesus uses in healing the paralytic of Mark 2: 9. But we have no warrant for saying that the cripple and the paralytic were one and the same person.

10. *You are not allowed to carry your bed on the Sabbath.* Cf. Jer. 17: 21, 'Bear no burden on the sabbath day'.

14. *leave your sinful ways, or you may suffer something worse.*
Some think that Jesus here attributes the man's sickness to his
sin. But is not Jesus rather saying, 'Crippling of body is bad
enough; but crippling of soul by sin leading to God's judgement is far worse'? ✳

JESUS AND THE FATHER

It was works of this kind done on the Sabbath that stirred 16
the Jews to persecute Jesus. He defended himself by 17
saying, 'My Father has never yet ceased his work, and I
am working too.' This made the Jews still more de- 18
termined to kill him, because he was not only breaking
the Sabbath, but, by calling God his own Father, he
claimed equality with God.

To this charge Jesus replied, 'In truth, in very truth I 19
tell you, the Son can do nothing by himself; he does only
what he sees the Father doing: what the Father does, the
Son does. For the Father loves the Son and shows him 20
all his works, and will show greater yet, to fill you with
wonder. As the Father raises the dead and gives them 21
life, so the Son gives life to men, as he determines. And 22
again, the Father does not judge anyone, but has given
full jurisdiction to the Son; it is his will that all should pay 23
the same honour to the Son as to the Father. To deny
honour to the Son is to deny it to the Father who sent
him.

'In very truth, anyone who gives heed to what I say 24
and puts his trust in him who sent me has hold of eternal
life, and does not come up for judgement, but has already
passed from death to life. In truth, in very truth I tell 25
you, a time is coming, indeed it is already here, when

the dead shall hear the voice of the Son of God, and all
26 who hear shall come to life. For as the Father has life-
giving power in himself, so has the Son, by the Father's
gift.

27 'As Son of Man, he has also been given the right to
28 pass judgement. Do not wonder at this, because the time
is coming when all who are in the grave shall hear his
29 voice and move forth: those who have done right will
rise to life; those who have done wrong will rise to hear
30 their doom. I cannot act by myself; I judge as I am
bidden, and my verdict is just, because my aim is not my
own will, but the will of him who sent me.

✴ In the verses which follow we learn how Jesus used to
defend his actions.

Much of the wording in this defence is clearly due to John.
But it would be wrong to imagine that it is all John's 'own
unaided work'. For if we seem often to hear John rather than
Jesus defining the relations between Father and Son, we find
that the basic themes can be traced back to the mind of Jesus
as we know it from the earlier Gospels.

The essence of Jesus' answer to the charge of Sabbath-
breaking is in verse 17. He is doing the will of the Lawgiver:
My Father has never yet ceased his work, he says, *and I am working
too*. According to Gen. 2: 3, God rested from his work on
the seventh day. A saying which so flatly contradicts this
must be accounted authentic. Jesus repudiates the idea that
God's rest from creation was idleness. My Father's creative
activity, he argues, never stops, even on the Sabbath, and it is
therefore I, not you, who rightly keep it. Rightly understood,
the Sabbath rest of the Father is the activity of love, so that in
merciful deeds done on the Sabbath the work of the Father
and the Son are at one.

In his apologia Jesus had called God *my Father* and had

followed it with an arrogant *and I*. This, a claim to be God's equal, replied the Jews, was blasphemy. Now, according to the rabbis, a *rebellious* son was said to 'make himself equal to his father'. It is this charge which Jesus now denies: so far from being a rebel, the soul of his sonship is obedience.

First, verse 19 f., he replies that a son can only do what he has learnt to do by watching his father, who out of love shows him how to work. So the Father will show the Son even greater things which will turn the Jews' present scoffing to wonder. He is thinking of the quickening of the spiritually dead.

Next, verse 21, we learn of two divine powers which the Father has given his incarnate Son. The first is that of *giving life*. Is physical or spiritual life meant? The answer is that, if verses 28 f. imply physical life, the main stress here is on spiritual.

The second power granted (verse 22) is that of *judgement*. *The Father does not judge anyone* means that he prejudices no man's chance of eternal life. On the contrary, he *has given full jurisdiction to the Son*, i.e. every man's destiny will be determined by his attitude to Christ. For God's purpose is that his Son, as his representative, should receive the same honour as himself. If honour is not given to the Son, the Father who sent him is dishonoured also.

With verse 24 Jesus introduces, as often after the formula *in very truth*, a further important thought. Those who accept his message and put their faith in his Divine Sender stand, even now, within the final order of God. They do not need to wait for the great Judge's acquittal on the last day; they already have eternal life. Cf. Rom. 8: 1.

In verse 25 another solemn affirmation follows. The time, he says, is coming—nay, it is already here—when dead men shall hear the Son of God's voice and *come to life*. He is thinking not of Resurrection Day but of the crisis created by his ministry. The dead are the spiritually dead who, by putting their faith in God's Son, experience the miracle of new life.

Such is the power—his own quickening power—which the Almighty Father has given to his Son.

And with this (verse 27) corresponds the power of judgement given to Christ as a Son of Man, i.e. being man, he knows what is in man.

It may be that in verses 28 f. we have the evangelist's comment, designed to correct any erroneous ideas that this present judgement excludes a Last Judgement. Such a final judgement there will be, and at it there will be *life* for *those who have done right* and doom for *those who have done wrong*. But if all men must appear before their Maker, we know already—see verse 24—that believers in Christ do not come up for judgement, having already passed from death to life. Verse 30 repeats that, as with his works, so it is with Christ's judgement. Because in judging he wholly depends on his Father, there can be no bias in him. ✳

WITNESSES TO CHRIST'S CLAIMS

31 'If I testify on my own behalf, that testimony does not
32 hold good. There is another who bears witness for me,
33 and I know that his testimony holds. Your messengers
    have been to John; you have his testimony to the truth.
34 Not that I rely on human testimony, but I remind you of
35 it for your own salvation. John was a lamp, burning
    brightly, and for a time you were ready to exult in his
36 light. But I rely on a testimony higher than John's.
    There is enough to testify that the Father has sent me, in
    the works my Father gave me to do and to finish—the
37 very works I have in hand. This testimony to me was
    given by the Father who sent me, although you never
38 heard his voice, or saw his form. But his word has found
    no home in you, for you do not believe the one whom
39 he sent. You study the scriptures diligently, supposing

that in having them you have eternal life; yet, although
their testimony points to me, you refuse to come to me   40
for that life.

'I do not look to men for honour. But with you it is   41,42
different, as I know well, for you have no love for God in
you. I have come accredited by my Father, and you have   43
no welcome for me; if another comes self-accredited you
will welcome him. How can you have faith so long as   44
you receive honour from one another, and care nothing
for the honour that comes from him who alone is God?
Do not imagine that I shall be your accuser at God's   45
tribunal. Your accuser is Moses, the very Moses on whom
you have set your hope. If you believed Moses you   46
would believe what I tell you, for it was about me that
he wrote. But if you do not believe what he wrote, how   47
are you to believe what I say?'

✶ To the claims that Jesus has just been making, the Jews
might reply, 'Why should we accept a man's own testimony
to himself? For all these claims we have only your own word.'
'If you had only my word for them', replies Jesus, 'that would
be so. But, in fact, *Another* [i.e. God] stands behind my
testimony and *bears* me *witness* through both my works and the
scriptures. Besides, you have the human testimony of John
who quite obviously impressed you for a while' (verses 31-40).

Then, turning defence into attack, Jesus declares that the
Jews' want of faith is due to moral causes. Because they care
more for man's approval than for God's—because their world
is man-centred, not God-centred—they fail to understand
their own scriptures which bear witness to himself (verses
41-7).

31. The law-courts—whether Jewish (Deut. 16: 6, 19: 15),
Greek or Roman—would not allow a man to act as witness in
his own case.

33. *Your messengers have been to John.* See 1: 19–31.

35. This is John's equivalent to Matt. 11: 7 ff., where Jesus, declaring John 'more than a prophet', names him the appointed herald of the New Order which is the kingdom of God. Here Jesus calls him a lamp, burning brightly and reminds the Jews that for a short time they had been glad to sun themselves, like gnats before a light, in the illumination John gave.

36. Jesus now turns from human testimony to divine— to his Father's. This consists in the *works*—his whole mission and message—God has given him to do. The appeal to his works reminds us of his reply to the Baptist's question from prison (Matt. 11: 4; Luke 7: 22).

37. The past tense (*was given*) probably refers to Christ's baptism (Mark 1: 11) when the heavenly voice said to him, 'Thou art my Son'. That voice the Jews did not hear, nor did they see the vision of the descending Spirit—*you never heard his voice, or saw his form.* How could they when his *word*—his whole revelation—*found no home* in them, through unbelief?

39. God's other testimony to his Son is given through their own scriptures, but again in vain. *You study the scriptures diligently*, says Jesus, using a verb which suggests intensive poring over the Torah or Law, *supposing that in having them you have eternal life.* Their rabbis certainly taught them so. One of them said, 'He who has gained for himself words of the Law has gained for himself the life of the world to come'.

40. Yet, says Jesus, *their testimony points to me.* Properly understood, the Old Testament points forward to Christ. Our Old Testament scholars produce books with titles like 'The Religion of the Old Testament', as though Old Testament religion existed in its own right. For the Jew this may be so. For the Christian the Old Testament finds its true meaning only in Christ and his Church.

41. Here begins Christ's counter-attack. In love with themselves, the Jews have no *love for God* in them. Otherwise, they would have welcomed him as God's *accredited* Messenger. But let *another self-accredited* person—some bogus Messiah—arise,

and they will acclaim him (as in A.D. 132 they acclaimed Bar Cochba).

44. A biting criticism found also in the earlier Gospels, e.g. Matt. 23: 5.

45–7. *Moses* means here the religion of the Law. The Jews have put their hope in it (as life-giving) instead of realizing that it points forward to Christ. But to suppose that the Law is life-giving is to find (as Paul did) that it exposes men as sinners. This exposure of sin makes Moses a prophet of the Gospel—which is the Good News of God's mercy to sinners. If the Jews had properly believed in Moses—if they had longed for forgiveness and eternal life—they would now be believing in Christ—which manifestly they are not. ✶

THE FEEDING OF THE FIVE THOUSAND

(In John 6: 1 Jesus crosses the Lake of Galilee. This is surprising since in chapter 5 the scene was Jerusalem. Some have therefore proposed to smooth out the geography of Jesus' movements by placing 6 after 4 and before 5. But 6: 37–41 presupposes the passage about the relation of Jesus to the Father in 5: 19–47. Since the theological order is therefore right, any reshuffling is suspect.)

Some time later Jesus withdrew to the farther shore of the **6** Sea of Galilee (or Tiberias), and a large crowd of people 2 followed who had seen the signs he performed in healing the sick. Then Jesus went up the hill-side and sat down 3 with his disciples. It was near the time of Passover, the 4 great Jewish festival. Raising his eyes and seeing a large 5 crowd coming towards him, Jesus said to Philip, 'Where are we to buy bread to feed these people?' This he said to 6 test him; Jesus himself knew what he meant to do. Philip 7 replied, 'Twenty pounds would not buy enough bread for

8 every one of them to have a little.' One of his disciples,
9 Andrew, the brother of Simon Peter, said to him, 'There
is a boy here who has five barley loaves and two fishes;
10 but what is that among so many?' Jesus said, 'Make
the people sit down.' There was plenty of grass there, so
11 the men sat down, about five thousand of them. Then
Jesus took the loaves, gave thanks, and distributed them
to the people as they sat there. He did the same with the
12 fishes, and they had as much as they wanted. When
everyone had had enough, he said to his disciples, 'Collect
13 the pieces left over, so that nothing may be lost.' This they
did, and filled twelve baskets with the pieces left uneaten
of the five barley loaves.

14   When the people saw the sign Jesus had performed, the
word went round, 'Surely this must be the prophet that
15 was to come into the world.' Jesus, aware that they meant
to come and seize him to proclaim him king, withdrew
again to the hills by himself.

* Two points must be made at the outset. (1) The evidence
suggests that John got his story of the feeding not from his
Synoptic predecessors but from the oral tradition of the
Church. (2) The order of events in John 6 (from the feeding
to Peter's confession) can be shown to be *historically superior*
to its counterpart in Mark 6-8.

But what are we to make of the miracle?

The miracle of the feeding is credible, but only on Christian
faith in the grand miracle of the Incarnation. 'Every evangelist,' writes William Temple, 'supposed our Lord to have
wrought a creative act: and, for myself, I have no doubt that
this is what occurred. This, however, is credible only if St
John is right in his doctrine of our Lord's Person. If the Lord
was indeed God incarnate, the story presents no insuperable

difficulties. But of course such a creative act is quite in-credible if he is other or less than God incarnate.' Those who do not share John's doctrine of Christ's person will 'rationalize' the miracle. They will say that what Jesus did was to set an example of sharing with his disciples which induced the crowd to produce their own food and share with each other.

But, miracle or no miracle, we have here something more than the mere multiplication of bread. This meal had *Messi-anic* significance. It was a sort of Galilean Lord's Supper, per-haps deliberately so contrived by Jesus at a time when the Passover was being celebrated in Jerusalem. Once Jesus had told a parable about a great supper which symbolized the kingdom of God (Luke 14: 15–24), and to which the invita-tion went out, 'Come, for all things are now ready'. Now Jesus acts out the parable, so that the bread becomes the Bread of the Kingdom or (in John's idiom) the Bread of Life.

1. *Tiberias.* The Galilean lake was sometimes called Tiberias after the mainly Gentile city which Herod Antipas had built on the lakeside in honour of the Emperor Tiberius.

4. *Passover, the great Jewish festival.* The second Passover of the ministry. But this is more than a chronological note: it is meant to supply a clue to the significance of the feeding.

5. In John it is Jesus (not the disciples, as in the Synoptics) who notices the lack of food.

7 f. *Philip* is shown as a business-like person, readier to rely on his own calculations than on unseen resources. Similarly, Andrew (mentioned thrice in this Gospel—1: 40, here and 12: 20) appears as a practical resourceful person, whose inter-ventions are always well timed.

9. *barley.* Barley bread was the food of the poor. The pickled fish probably served as a relish.

10. *There was plenty of grass there.* Cf. Mark 6: 39, 'on the green grass'. It was April and spring-time.

11. *Jesus took the loaves, gave thanks, and distributed them.* This was the regular Jewish prayer of thanksgiving and blessing offered by the head of the house, or the host, before a meal

began. The Church soon came to apply the same verbs to the Lord's Supper.

12. This command is only in John. God's bounty is not to be wasted.

14 f. *Surely this must be the prophet,* i.e. predicted in Deut. 18: 15. At 1: 21 the prophet is distinguished from the Messiah. Here, as verse 15 shows, he is identified with him.

Clearly Messianic excitement with political tendencies was running very high at this time. What Jesus saw on the shore was an army without a commander, a leaderless mob, a danger to themselves and to everyone else. John's comment *they meant to come and seize him to proclaim him king* (i.e. the Messianic king) explains why the five thousand men were arranged in quasi-military formation ('a hundred rows of fifty each', Mark 6: 40) and why Jesus 'made' (Mark 6: 45) his disciples depart to the other side of the Lake while he himself stayed behind to disperse the crowd. A 'revolt in the desert' was threatening.

This, the third sign, will be interpreted in the discourse about the Bread of Life. But before this happens, the sequel to the feeding is related. ✳

STORM ON THE LAKE AND THE MORNING AFTER

16,17 At nightfall his disciples went down to the sea, got into their boat, and pushed off to cross the water to Capernaum. Darkness had already fallen, and Jesus had not yet
18 joined them. By now a strong wind was blowing and
19 the sea grew rough. When they had rowed about three or four miles they saw Jesus walking on the sea and
20 approaching the boat. They were terrified, but he called
21 out, 'It is I; do not be afraid.' Then they were ready to take him aboard, and immediately the boat reached the land they were making for.

Next morning the crowd was standing on the opposite 22
shore. They had seen only one boat there, and Jesus, they
knew, had not embarked with his disciples, who had gone
away without him. Boats from Tiberias, however, came 23
ashore near the place where the people had eaten the
bread over which the Lord gave thanks. When the people 24
saw that neither Jesus nor his disciples were any longer
there, they themselves went aboard these boats and made
for Capernaum in search of Jesus. They found him on the 25
other side. 'Rabbi,' they said, 'when did you come here?'
Jesus replied, 'In very truth I know that you have come 26
looking for me because your hunger was satisfied with
the loaves you ate, not because you saw signs. You must 27
work, not for this perishable food, but for the food that
lasts, the food of eternal life.

✳ As in the Synoptics, the story of the storm follows immediately after the feeding. But the differences between John's
version and Mark 6: 45–52 make it very unlikely that John
borrowed the story from Mark.

As Mark tells the story, a miracle is clearly intended. But
miracles should not be unnecessarily multiplied; and in John's
account no miracle need be involved. To be sure, the N.E.B.'s
walking on the sea (verse 19) assumes one. But if John's Greek
has the same meaning here as it has in 21: 1, it should be
rendered 'by the sea', i.e. on the shore or, at most, in the surf.
Nor does the mention of *three or four miles* rowing mean that
the boat was then in mid-lake. If the disciples crossed the
northern (and narrower) part of the Lake, a row of three or
four miles would bring them close to the Capernaum shore.
This, according to John, is what it did.

What we have here then is the story of a memorable reunion between Jesus and his disciples. After the Messianic
crisis Jesus had sent the disciples ahead in the boat, intending

to make his way along the lake-side and rejoin them later. This
he did in unforgettable circumstances. After their buffeting in
the storm, it is small wonder that the disciples were alarmed
to see the figure of Jesus suddenly loom out of the darkness in
the surf breaking on the western shore. Nor is it surprising
that in the retelling such an incident grew into a miracle. For
early Christian preachers the story must have made a splendid
illustration, from 'the days of his flesh', of the ever-present
Saviour.

17. *Jesus had not yet joined them.* He did so, according to
Mark 6: 48, between 3 and 6 a.m.

Verses 22–4 tell how the crowds caught up again with
Jesus and his disciples. Left on the eastern shore, the crowds
noted that the one boat available for Jesus and his men had
been used by the disciples to cross the Lake. When in the
morning Jesus too had gone and the disciples had not come
back for him, they guessed correctly that Jesus had rejoined
his disciples at Capernaum. Fortunately, other boats turned
up from Tiberias, and in these the crowds crossed to Capernaum where they found Jesus. *

THE BREAD OF LIFE

'This food the Son of Man will give you, for he it is upon
28 whom the Father has set the seal of his authority.' 'Then
what must we do', they asked him, 'if we are to work as
29 God would have us work?' Jesus replied, 'This is the
work that God requires: believe in the one whom he has
sent.'

30   They said, 'What sign can you give us to see, so that we
31 may believe you? What is the work you do? Our
ancestors had manna to eat in the desert; as Scripture says,
32 "He gave them bread from heaven to eat."' Jesus
answered, 'I tell you this: the truth is, not that Moses

gave you the bread from heaven, but that my Father
gives you the real bread from heaven. The bread that 33
God gives comes down from heaven and brings life to the
world.' They said to him, 'Sir, give us this bread now and 34
always.' Jesus said to them, 'I am the bread of life. Who- 35
ever comes to me shall never be hungry, and whoever
believes in me shall never be thirsty. But you, as I said, 36
do not believe although you have seen. All that the 37
Father gives me will come to me, and the man who comes
to me I will never turn away. I have come down from 38
heaven, not to do my own will, but the will of him who
sent me. It is his will that I should not lose even one of all 39
that he has given me, but raise them all up on the last
day. For it is my Father's will that everyone who looks 40
upon the Son and puts his faith in him shall possess eternal
life; and I will raise him up on the last day.'

* The long discourse on the Bread of Life, without parallel
in the earlier Gospels (unless it be Mark 6: 51; 8: 14–21), is a
deliberate attempt to declare the true meaning of an important
episode in the Gospel story. 'Jesus fed the multitude; and he
provided his action with its proper meaning. He is the answer
to the desire of men for food and for a King, just as he is the
fulfilment of the Jewish Law and the Jewish scriptures' (Hoskyns). Doubtless the discourse was mainly shaped by the
evangelist. But when we remember (1) that Jesus was speaking
at Passover time and that many ideas in the discourse—bread,
manna, heavenly food—figured also in the Jewish Passover
ritual, and (2) that, later, according to the Synoptics, Jesus was
to interpret the Passover bread and wine of his own person,
we cannot dismiss it simply as 'Johannine theologizing'. 'John
is setting forth its veritable meaning, and not some speculation
of his own about it' (Hoskyns).
Jesus begins by rebuking the crowd who had followed him.

Their interest in him was carnal, not spiritual: they were toiling after him in hope of another free meal when they ought to have been working for the food that lasts—the food of eternal life.

The crowd, hearing Jesus bid them work (and having a religion which set much store by 'works'), ask: 'What work does God require of us?' only to be told that the one work God requires is faith—faith in his Messenger.

Sensing that he is referring to himself, they retort: 'What work can you do to justify our faith in you?' In other words, if they are to believe in him, he must produce a sign—like bread from heaven (Ps. 78: 24). 'Show us manna falling from heaven as Moses let our ancestors see it falling in the desert' (Exod. 16: 12–21). (The Jews believed that the renewal of the manna would be one of Messiah's chief gifts in the New Age.)

Jesus (verse 32) finds two errors in their words. First, it was not Moses but God who gave the manna; and, second, the manna was corruptible bread, not the bread from heaven. The *real bread* from heaven—the bread of which earthly bread is but a symbol—the Father is now giving them. *The bread that God gives,* he says, *comes down from heaven and brings life to the world.* These words (verse 33) could be translated personally: 'is he who comes down from heaven'. The crowd, taking them impersonally, and thinking of the previous day's plenty, ask for a perpetual supply of this bread (cf. 4: 15).

Thereupon (verse 35) Jesus reveals himself: *I am the bread of life.* The phrase means both 'living bread' and 'life-giving bread'. Jesus does not merely bestow a gift; he is himself the gift; and the man who receives it will never hunger any more.

Then (verse 36) Jesus warns them not to lose this gift through unbelief. The gift involves coming to him; and (he says) before men can come, God must will their coming. Any true followers he has are his Father's gift to him, and he will refuse none who come. His sole aim is to do not his own will but his Father's, and this is that he should lose none, but *raise them all up on the last day.*

27. *the Son of Man.* Jesus does not say 'Messiah'—verse 15 explains why—but Son of Man, a title which, to the initiated, hints at the secret of his person.

28 f. This is as sharp a statement of 'faith and works' as any to be found in Paul. It was in fact the answer Paul gave to the Philippian jailer (Acts 16: 30 f.).

31. One Jewish rabbi said: 'What did the first Redeemer [Moses]? He brought down the manna. And the last Redeemer will bring down the manna.'

39 f. These verses remind us that, though John thinks of eternal life as a present blessing, he does not reject the doctrine of a final consummation. ✳

THE MURMURING OF THE JEWS

At this the Jews began to murmur disapprovingly be- 41 cause he said, 'I am the bread which came down from heaven.' They said, 'Surely this is Jesus son of Joseph; 42 we know his father and mother. How can he now say, "I have come down from heaven"?' Jesus answered, 43 'Stop murmuring among yourselves. No man can come 44 to me unless he is drawn by the Father who sent me; and I will raise him up on the last day. It is written in the 45 prophets: "And they shall all be taught by God." Everyone who has listened to the Father and learned from him comes to me.

'I do not mean that anyone has seen the Father. He 46 who has come from God has seen the Father, and he alone. In truth, in very truth I tell you, the believer 47 possesses eternal life. I am the bread of life. Your 48,49 forefathers ate the manna in the desert and they are dead. I am speaking of the bread that comes down from 50 heaven, which a man may eat, and never die. I am that 51 living bread which has come down from heaven: if anyone eats this bread he shall live for ever. Moreover, the bread which I will give is my own flesh; I give it for the life of the world.'

* Jesus' lofty claims are now challenged by the Jews on the ground of his lowly origin (cf. Mark 6: 3): *Surely this is Jesus son of Joseph: we know his father and mother.* They think that, knowing his parents, they know all there is to be known about him. Replying (verse 44), Jesus raises the discussion from this earthly to a heavenly level. Belief is not something a man achieves by his own unaided effort (cf. Christ's words to Peter in Matt. 16: 17); the initiative always lies with divine grace, or, as he puts it, only the Father can *draw* a man to such a momentous step. And he quotes Isa. 54: 13, *they shall all be taught by God,* where the stress falls on God as the ultimate cause of a man's belief.

In verse 46 (a sort of 'aside') we learn that this revelation does not come by direct vision but only by faith in the heaven-sent Mediator, and this teaching concludes with Jesus repeating (verses 47–50) some truths already uttered. The life of faith does not earn eternal life; it is it. The old manna could not avert physical death: the new manna brings new life over which death has no power. And that new bread is himself. *I am that living bread which has come down from heaven* (verse 51). The reference to the Incarnation, veiled in verse 33, now becomes plain. But one momentous statement yet remains: *the bread which I will give is my own flesh; I give it for the life of the world.* Here we pass from what Christ *is* to what he *gives*—or, rather, *will give.* His gift of life involves his death; and it is not for a nation but for a *world.* The saying prophetically links Galilee with Golgotha, the Incarnation with the Atonement. And with the Atonement goes the Lord's Supper clearly in view in the following verses.

44. *unless he is drawn by the Father.* This is the bright side of the doctrine of predestination.

46. Cf. Matt. 11: 27 where Jesus declares that he alone can impart to his chosen ones his unique knowledge of God.

51. This is John's version of 'This is my body, which is for you' (1 Cor. 11: 24). John changes 'body' to 'flesh': compare 1: 14. In this verse the evangelist anticipates the institution of the Lord's Supper, which is possibly one reason why he does not record it in chapters 13–17. ✳

THE FLESH AND THE BLOOD OF THE SON OF MAN

This led to a fierce dispute among the Jews. 'How can 52 this man give us his flesh to eat?' they said. Jesus replied, 53 'In truth, in very truth I tell you, unless you eat the flesh of the Son of Man and drink his blood you can have no life in you. Whoever eats my flesh and drinks my blood 54 possesses eternal life, and I will raise him up on the last day. My flesh is real food; my blood is real drink. 55 Whoever eats my flesh and drinks my blood dwells con- 56 tinually in me and I dwell in him. As the living Father 57 sent me, and I live because of the Father, so he who eats me shall live because of me. This is the bread which came 58 down from heaven; and it is not like the bread which our fathers ate: they are dead, but whoever eats this bread shall live for ever.'

✳ Jesus' words set the Jews in a wrangle. Is he advocating cannibalism of some kind? Jesus replies that, unless they eat the flesh and drink the blood of the Son of Man, they cannot have eternal life. This is sacramental language. To *eat* and *drink* means to assimilate into one's own being; the *flesh* and *blood of the Son of Man* mean Christ's life set free by death for wider purposes. And so, to eat and drink of them must mean to make one's own the virtue of his sacrifice—to be so united to the living Crucified as to share in the divine, eternal life he bestows.

My flesh, he says (verse 55), *is real food; my blood is real drink.*
The contrast is doubtless with those transitory things with
which men try to satisfy themselves. To share in this real food
and drink is to have union with Christ by mutual indwelling
(a theme to recur often in the Farewell Discourses). *As the*
living Father sent me, and I live because of the Father, Jesus concludes, *so he who eats me shall live because of me* (verse 57). Such
communion has in it the secret of everlasting life. And with
this description of himself as life-giver he ends his discourse.

All this, we learn (verse 59), was teaching given at Capernaum *in synagogue* (so we say 'in church'). But cannot the
discourse be taken as addressed to the Church in all ages, and
not only to Jesus' own hearers? Yes, and this is John's inten-
tion. His theme—that Christ is God's answer to men's hunger
for bread—has as its background the first Lord's Supper in
Galilee. But, with the Spirit's help, John has so worked out
the true issue, which is faith and unbelief, that the world and the
Church, faced by the same issue as the Galileans, may overhear
and decide. ✱

REACTION—AND CONFESSION

59 This was spoken in synagogue when Jesus was teaching
60 in Capernaum. Many of his disciples on hearing it
exclaimed, 'This is more than we can stomach! Why
61 listen to such words?' Jesus was aware that his disciples
were murmuring about it and asked them, 'Does this
62 shock you? What if you see the Son of Man ascending
63 to the place where he was before? The spirit alone gives
life; the flesh is of no avail; the words which I have spoken
64 to you are both spirit and life. And yet there are some of
you who have no faith.' For Jesus knew all along who
65 were without faith and who was to betray him. So he
said, 'This is why I told you that no one can come to me
unless it has been granted to him by the Father.'

From that time on, many of his disciples withdrew and 66
no longer went about with him. So Jesus asked the 67
Twelve, 'Do you also want to leave me?' Simon Peter 68
answered him, 'Lord, to whom shall we go? Your
words are words of eternal life. We have faith, and we 69
know that you are the Holy One of God.' Jesus answered, 70
'Have I not chosen you, all twelve? Yet one of you is a
devil.' He meant Judas, son of Simon Iscariot. He it was 71
who would betray him, and he was one of the Twelve.

✻ This, the final scene in Christ's Galilean ministry, is one of
failure. (Yet, 'failure' and 'success' are misleading words in
any account of Jesus' work, since all happens according to
God's will.) It is also the record of judgement, in which the
sifting descends even to the disciple-band. First, we learn how
Christ's words *shocked* many; and then how, when many followers deserted him, the Twelve through Peter confessed him
to be the Messiah and the Bearer of eternal life.

Consider, first, the difficult verses 60-3. Christ's words
about eating and drinking the flesh and blood of the Son of
Man shock his hearers by their 'materialism'. Aware of their
unease, he therefore points them to the future, to his completed work, as the solution. When the Son of Man has
ascended, and the Spirit the life-giver, who now rests on him
only, comes to his followers, all will be plain. Then those who
eat his flesh and drink his blood—assimilate the virtue of his
life and death—will receive the Spirit, and, with it, life. *The
spirit alone gives life; the flesh is of no avail; the words which I have
spoken to you are both spirit and life.* The contrast here is not
between flesh and spirit but between dead flesh and living
flesh. By itself flesh is flesh and avails nothing. But if it is
filled by God's Spirit, it becomes both alive and life-giving.
As the incarnate Word is living flesh in the power of the
Spirit, so the words of the Son of God give life to what is dead
and profitless, and are therefore *spirit and life*.

Next (verse 64) we learn that the unbelief of some of his followers, and even the desertion of Judas, were known to Jesus beforehand. This was confirmed when many of them *withdrew and no longer went about with him* (verse 66). (We may contrast this scene with that in verse 15. Then, five thousand men excitedly intent on making him king; now, only twelve men, who will soon be eleven, standing beside him.) As Jesus watches the deserters on their way, there is infinite pathos in his *Do you also want to leave me?* (verse 62). Thereupon Peter, speaking for the band, confesses Christ to be the only Saviour of man. It is John's version of Peter's confession (Mark 8: 29). Christ's words are *words of eternal life*, because they both announce and convey it. If Peter calls him *the Holy One of God*, this is another way of saying 'the Messiah' (Mark 1: 24).

But even this sublime confession (so admirably expressing the faith of true Christians in all ages) is no warrant that all the remaining twelve are loyal. One in fact is already doing Satan's work for him. For Jesus, John says (verses 64, 71), had no illusions about Judas; he went to his death well aware of the conspiracy of evil against him.

60. *This is more than we can stomach!* Literally, 'this is a hard saying': not hard to understand, but hard to accept.

71. *Judas, son of Simon Iscariot.* Both Judas and his father were called *Iscariot*, 'man of Kerioth' (see Jer. 48: 24; Amos 2: 2). ✳

The Great Controversy

JESUS IN JERUSALEM AT THE FEAST OF TABERNACLES

7 AFTERWARDS Jesus went about in Galilee. He wished to avoid Judaea because the Jews were looking for a 2 chance to kill him. As the Jewish Feast of Tabernacles 3 was close at hand, his brothers said to him, 'You should

leave this district and go into Judaea, so that your disciples there may see the great things you are doing. Surely no 4 one can hope to be in the public eye if he works in seclusion. If you really are doing such things as these, show yourself to the world.' For even his brothers were 5 not believers in him. Jesus said to them, 'The right time 6 for me has not yet come, but any time is right for you. The world cannot hate you; but it hates me for exposing 7 the wickedness of its ways. Go to the festival yourselves. 8 I am not going up to this festival because the right time for me has not yet come.' With this answer he stayed 9 behind in Galilee.

Later, when his brothers had gone to the festival, he 10 went up himself, not publicly, but almost in secret. The 11 Jews were looking for him at the festival and asking, 'Where is he?', and there was much whispering about 12 him in the crowds. 'He is a good man', said some. 'No,' said others, 'he is leading the people astray.' However, 13 no one talked about him openly, for fear of the Jews.

⁂ The theme of chapters 7 and 8 is Christ manifesting himself to Israel as life and light, only to be rejected. The background is Jerusalem at its most popular religious feast, Tabernacles. The scene is full of local colour, and all is direct personal encounter.

Afterwards Jesus went about in Galilee…the Feast of Tabernacles was close at hand. Evidently Jesus conducted an itinerant ministry in Galilee for some six months between the April of the second Passover (6: 4) and the October feast of Tabernacles. When eventually he went up to Jerusalem for the feast, he left Galilee for good (cf. Mark 9: 30; 10: 1 for a similar secret journey). In the following chapters he is found in or near Jerusalem until 10: 40 when he goes to Transjordan.

Tabernacles, or 'Booths' (see Lev. 23; Deut. 16 and Ezra 3), was the third, the last and the most joyous of the three main Jewish festivals. Originally a 'Harvest-home' to celebrate the ingathering of the various crops, it had acquired an 'Exodus' meaning through its linkage with the time when God made the children of Israel dwell in tents after their deliverance from Egypt. So for eight days the pilgrims dwelt in tents temporarily erected in the streets or on the roofs of the city.

As the feast approaches, Christ's brothers suggest to him that his proper place is not in Galilee but in Jerusalem. There his *disciples*, i.e. presumably his Jerusalem supporters, should get the chance of seeing his wonderful powers. The brethren, though they do not believe in their divine brother, do not deny his wonder-working, but they insist (verse 4) that, if he wishes fame and following, the wider world of the capital is the proper place for its display. It is, in kind, the same suggestion as the devil made in the Temptation (Matt. 4: 5–7): dazzle the people into belief in you. By their plea to use the world's methods they betray that they too are 'of the world' and do not understand Christ's mission. When he replies (verses 6 ff.) that the *right time* for him has not yet come, he means the time appointed for him by his Father: only at his signal may he move. For his brothers, however, *any time is right. Go to the festival yourselves*, says Jesus, *I am not going up to this festival.*

Yet, two verses later, we read that Jesus went up half-way through it. Was Jesus guilty of dissembling? (Some scribes, feeling the difficulty, changed the *not* of verse 8 into *not yet*, in concern for Jesus' reputation.) This explanation can be ruled out at once. What Jesus means in verse 8 is: 'I am not going up merely at your order; I must wait my Father's bidding.' That he went later means that the signal came. But note that he went *not publicly, but almost in secret* (verse 10): not in open caravan with the other pilgrims but by himself, unobtrusively, to do what God bade him to do.

Arriving in the capital, he finds the crowds whispering in corners about him, some favourably, some unfavourably; but *fear of the Jews*—of the religious authorities—prevents any open talk.

8. Possibly the Greek verb meaning 'to go up' carries here not its usual geographical sense but the *spiritual* one it has at 3: 13; 6: 62 and 20: 17. It would then refer to Christ's ascent to the Father by way of the cross: 'I am not going up (to my Father) at this feast.' It was at the third Passover of the ministry that Jesus 'went up' in this sense. ✶

CONTROVERSY IN THE TEMPLE

When the festival was already half over, Jesus went up to the temple and began to teach. The Jews were astonished: 'How is it', they said, 'that this untrained man has such learning?' Jesus replied, 'The teaching that I give is not my own; it is the teaching of him who sent me. Whoever has the will to do the will of God shall know whether my teaching comes from him or is merely my own. Anyone whose teaching is merely his own, aims at honour for himself. But if a man aims at the honour of him who sent him he is sincere, and there is nothing false in him.

'Did not Moses give you the Law? Yet you all break it. Why are you trying to kill me?' The crowd answered, 'You are possessed! Who wants to kill you?' Jesus replied, 'Once only have I done work on the Sabbath, and you are all taken aback. But consider: Moses gave you the law of circumcision (not that it originated with Moses but with the patriarchs) and you circumcise on the Sabbath. Well then, if a child is circumcised on the Sabbath to avoid breaking the Law of Moses, why are you indignant with me for giving health on the Sabbath

24 to the whole of a man's body? Do not judge superficially, but be just in your judgements.'

✻ Mid-way through the festival, i.e. about the fourth day, *Jesus went up to the temple and began to teach.* The *right time* for him (verse 6) had come, not to dazzle men by miracle but to proclaim God's will in the metropolis of Israel. But, as he does so, his gifts as a teacher astonish the Jewish authorities: after all, as everybody knew, the man from Galilee had never had a rabbinical education. Jesus' reply is that he has had a much greater teacher—he is a pupil of his Father. Does any doubt this? Then let him put his will in line with God's will, and Jesus' teaching will find a confirming echo in his conscience: obedience is the source of spiritual vision. Moreover, it is characteristic of a man who merely speaks his own mind, to glorify himself. But Jesus' motives are quite disinterested, concerned as he is not with his own honour but with God's (verses 14–18).

Then (verse 19) he moves to attack. 'Did not Moses give you the law about the Sabbath?' he asks, 'And yet none of you is keeping it. You are plotting to kill me. Is not this a flagrant breach of it?' 'It is only your disordered mind,' replies the crowd, 'that makes you imagine people want to kill you.' Then Jesus presses home his attack, on the basis of the Law: 'I did one work—of healing—on the Sabbath,' he says, 'and you protest yourselves horrified by my conduct. Let us take together another look at Moses' laws. Moses laid down the circumcision law (Lev. 12: 3). He also laid down the law about the Sabbath. Suppose these two laws clash. When this happens, the Sabbath law, as you know, gives way to the circumcision one. This orders the doing of this *work* on the eighth day after birth, Sabbath though it be. But if what affects one member may be done on the Sabbath, surely a work which gives health to a man's whole body may be done on the holy day.'

What Jesus had done was to put right not one member only

but the whole man. This surely was the true spirit of the Law;
and to call it Sabbath-breaking was to judge very superficially.
'Don't judge by looks,' says Jesus, 'but be fair.' It is the last
word in the controversy caused by his healing of the cripple.

22. *not that it originated with Moses but with the patriarchs.*
The law about circumcision was written down by Moses, but
its origin goes back to the patriarchs, in fact to Abraham
(Gen. 17: 10). *

CAN THIS BE THE MESSIAH?

At this some of the people of Jerusalem began to say, 'Is 25
not this the man they want to put to death? And here 26
he is, speaking openly, and they have not a word to say
to him. Can it be that our rulers have actually decided
that this is the Messiah? And yet we know where this 27
man comes from, but when the Messiah appears no one
is to know where he comes from.' Thereupon Jesus cried 28
aloud as he taught in the temple, 'No doubt you know
me; no doubt you know where I come from. Yet I have
not come of my own accord. I was sent by the One
who truly is, and him you do not know. I know him 29
because I come from him and he it is who sent me.' At 30
this they tried to seize him, but no one laid a hand on him
because his appointed hour had not yet come. Yet among 31
the people many believed in him. 'When the Messiah
comes,' they said, 'is it likely that he will perform more
signs than this man?'

The Pharisees overheard these mutterings of the people 32
about him, so the chief priests and the Pharisees sent
temple police to arrest him. Then Jesus said, 'For a little 33
longer I shall be with you; then I am going away to him

34 who sent me. You will look for me, but you will not
35 find me. Where I am, you cannot come.' So the Jews
said to one another, 'Where does he intend to go, that
we should not be able to find him? Will he go to the
Dispersion among the Greeks, and teach the Greeks?
36 What did he mean by saying, "You will look for me, but
you will not find me. Where I am, you cannot come"?'

✶ The residents of Jerusalem, puzzled by their rulers' inde-
cision, begin to surmise that Jesus may indeed be the Messiah.
But they are quite unsure: have they not been taught that
Messiah's coming is to be veiled in mystery, whereas no such
obscurity surrounds this man whose origin and antecedents
they know: Nazareth in Galilee, a quite 'un-Messianic' birthplace? To this Jesus replies in effect: 'Your information about
me, so far as it goes, is correct, but irrelevant. In one sense you
know me; in a deeper sense you do not. For I am come from
God, and so, for you, because you do not know God, my
origin is a mystery.' A highly provocative thing to say to
any Jerusalem Jew proud in his possession of Law and Temple!
No wonder they tried to arrest him—an attempt which mis-
carried because the people were of two minds (verses 25-31).

Popular whispering about Jesus now compels the Sanhedrin, the supreme Jewish religious council, to make the
next move through their temple police. When Jesus tells them,
rather sadly, that he will soon be going where they cannot
come (i.e. to his heavenly Father, via the cross) they misunderstand him to mean that he is going to visit Gentile
lands. They prophesy more truly than they know. Yet even
this suggestion does not wholly convince them: a vague
sense lingers that Christ's words hold unfathomed depths
(verses 32-6).

27. For the doctrine of the Unknown Messiah see the note
on 1: 31. A rabbinical saying had it that, 'three things come
unexpectedly: Messiah, a godsend, and a scorpion'.

31. The Messiah was expected to work miracles. So, in the Synoptics, the Baptist, hearing of Jesus' mighty works, inquires through messengers, 'Are you the one who is to come?', i.e. the Messiah (Luke 7: 18 f.).

33. *a little longer*. The brief interval before the cross and his return to the Father.

35. *Will he go to the Dispersion among the Greeks* (i.e. to the Jews who lived among Greek peoples) *and teach the Greeks?* (i.e. the pagan Greeks themselves). They suggest that he is not only planning a visit to his Jewish brethren scattered in Gentile lands (Alexandria, Rome, etc.), but is even proposing a mission to those who by birth are not Jews at all. ✻

THE LAST DAY OF THE FEAST

On the last and greatest day of the festival Jesus stood and cried aloud, 'If anyone is thirsty let him come to me; whoever believes in me, let him drink.' As Scripture says, 'Streams of living water shall flow out from within him.' He was speaking of the Spirit which believers in him would receive later; for the Spirit had not yet been given, because Jesus had not yet been glorified. 37 38 39

On hearing this some of the people said, 'This must certainly be the expected prophet.' Others said, 'This is the Messiah.' Others again, 'Surely the Messiah is not to come from Galilee? Does not Scripture say that the Messiah is to be of the family of David, from David's village of Bethlehem?' Thus he caused a split among the people. Some were for seizing him, but no one laid hands on him. 40 41 42 43 44

The temple police came back to the chief priests and Pharisees, who asked, 'Why have you not brought him?' 'No man', they answered, 'ever spoke as this man 45 46

47 speaks.' The Pharisees retorted, 'Have you too been
48 misled? Is there a single one of our rulers who has
49 believed in him, or of the Pharisees? As for this rabble,
which cares nothing for the Law, a curse is on them.'
50 Then one of their number, Nicodemus (the man who had
51 once visited Jesus), intervened. 'Does our law', he asked
them, 'permit us to pass judgement on a man unless we
have first given him a hearing and learned the facts?'
52 'Are you a Galilean too?' they retorted. 'Study the
scriptures and you will find that prophets do not come
from Galilee.'

✻ A high point in the ritual of Tabernacles was the pouring
out in the Temple court of a golden pitcher of water from the
Siloam Pool. This libation (which may have been originally a
symbolic prayer for rain) was held to symbolize the future
outpouring of the Spirit in the Messianic Age. On the last
day of the festival, named *great* because it was celebrated with
all the dignity of a Sabbath, Jesus uses this ritual to claim that
in himself will be found the fulfilment of all the ritual represented. He was referring, comments John, to the gift of the
Spirit after his ascension.

This dramatic claim makes some think that he is the Messiah;
others think that Scripture proves a Galilean Messiah an ab-
surdity; others want to arrest him. The Temple police (cf.
verse 32) report to their superiors that his unique mastery of
speech makes arrest impossible. And Nicodemus pleads for a
fair hearing before they condemn him.

37. *The last...day* was probably the eighth day.

38 f. The words of Jesus are a claim to be the dispenser of
the water of life. But the Scripture which John cites has
proved a puzzle. It looks like a free citation of verse 8 of
Zech. 14, a chapter which was the appointed lesson for the
feast of Tabernacles (cf. Zech. 14: 16 with its reference to 'the
feast of tabernacles'). But in John's mind is also the concept

of Jesus as the rock in the wilderness which, when smitten, brought forth water (Exod. 17: 6; cf. 1 Cor. 10: 4). It is out of Christ, John says, that the living waters will flow. The later picture of water flowing from the side of the crucified Saviour (19: 34) makes it almost certain that the Scripture is here applied to Christ, and not to the believer. This interpretation makes a good connexion with the next verse (39), where John tells us that Jesus was foretelling the gift of the Spirit, a prophecy which came true after his ascension. *For the Spirit had not yet been given*, he says, *because Jesus had not yet been glorified*. The Spirit was to take the place of Jesus (14: 16) and could not therefore be given till he was *glorified*, i.e. crucified and exalted. Christ's death was both the condition of his glory and of his full spiritual activity. Cf. Luke 12: 49 f. for the same thought.

40. *the expected prophet*. See Deut. 18: 15.

42. According to the Old Testament, the Messiah was to be born of David's line (2 Sam. 7: 12 f.; Isa. 11: 1; Jer. 23: 5, etc.), and Bethlehem where David was born, to be his birthplace (1 Sam. 16: 1, 4; Micah 5: 2).

49. Since piety rested on knowledge of the Law, the rabbis despised the *rabble* for their ignorance of it. Rabbi Hillel said, 'No vulgar person is pious'.

50. *one of their number* means that Nicodemus was a member of the Sanhedrin. On his first visit to Jesus he had come by night, and he does not yet come into the open. The most he can rise to now is a mild protest for a fair hearing for Jesus, i.e. a legal ground for deferring judgement. But his plea is greeted by sarcasm, 'Are you a Galilean too? Everybody knows that Galilee does not produce prophets.' Yet Jonah, Nahum and possibly Hosea came from Galilee.

For the story of Jesus and the adulteress which, traditionally, is John 7: 53 — 8: 11 but, in fact, is an oral tradition (and one of priceless value) see 'An Incident in the Temple' at the end of the commentary (p. 199). *

JESUS THE LIGHT OF THE WORLD

8 12 Once again Jesus addressed the people: 'I am the light of the world. No follower of mine shall wander in the 13 dark; he shall have the light of life.' The Pharisees said to him, 'You are witness in your own cause; your 14 testimony is not valid.' Jesus replied, 'My testimony is valid, even though I do bear witness about myself; because I know where I come from, and where I am going. You do not know either where I come from or where I 15 am going. You judge by worldly standards. I pass judge- 16 ment on no man, but if I do judge, my judgement is valid because it is not I alone who judge, but I and he who 17 sent me. In your own law it is written that the testimony 18 of two witnesses is valid. Here am I, a witness in my own cause, and my other witness is the Father who sent me.' 19 They asked, 'Where is your father?' Jesus replied, 'You know neither me nor my Father; if you knew me you would know my Father as well.'

20 These words were spoken by Jesus in the treasury as he taught in the temple. Yet no one arrested him, because his hour had not yet come.

✻ The second stage in the debate at Tabernacles deals with Jesus' origin and nature, his relation to the Father, and the judgement falling on the unbelieving Jews.

Light was a dominant symbol of the Tabernacles festival. A high point in the ritual came with the lighting of the four great candelabra in the Court of the Women (where the Treasury was) to commemorate the Pillar of Fire in the Wilderness (Exod. 13: 21). We are told that so brilliant was the illumination it lit up every courtyard in Jerusalem. This is the background of Jesus' claim.

In the Old Testament light is a favourite symbol for God in his saving and revealing action—witness Ps. 27: 1 and 43: 3. Moreover, traditionally, 'Light' was one of Messiah's names; and Isaiah had declared that the Lord's Servant was to be 'a light to the Gentiles' (Isa. 49: 6). Turning to the New Testament, we find Jesus calling his chosen men 'light for all the world' (Matt. 5: 14). From this it is a short step to the majestic claim that Jesus now makes—that he, and he alone, can savingly irradiate the dark mystery of men's existence and give their life meaning, purpose and destiny.

When the Pharisees reply (verse 13) that a man's unsupported testimony to himself is invalid, Jesus justifies it by declaring that only superficially is it such; for (a) he alone knows his origin and destiny; and (b) his witness is not unsupported, since he has also the witness of his Sender. He may be a witness in his own cause, but 'unseen within the shadow' stands the other needed witness—his heavenly Father. They retort, *Where is your Father?* In other words, produce your other witness. They want a theophany (a manifestation of God) on the spot. Jesus can but reply that his hearers' want of faith and trust precludes the revelation of God that might otherwise have been theirs. 'If you really were in spiritual communion with me' says Jesus in effect, 'you would know my Father too' (verses 14–19).

Here (verse 20) John adds an unexpected note of locality. The words were spoken *in the treasury*, that part of the Women's Court where stood the thirteen funnel-shaped boxes to receive the people's offerings. (Into one of them the widow put her farthing, Mark 12: 41.) Thus it was practically next door to the chamber where the Sanhedrin met, within easy earshot of his enemies. *Yet no one arrested him*, comments John. The reason was not the clash of human wills and motives but the divine purpose.

17. *In your own law.* The evidence of two persons is valid (Deut. 17: 6; Num. 35: 30).

19. Here, as in the Bible generally, 'knowing God' means

not theoretical knowledge of God but spiritual communion with him. ✻

WARNINGS OF COMING DOOM

21 Again he said to them, 'I am going away. You will look for me, but you will die in your sin; where I am going 22 you cannot come.' The Jews then said, 'Perhaps he will kill himself: is that what he means when he says, "Where 23 I am going you cannot come"?' So Jesus continued, 'You belong to this world below, I to the world above. 24 Your home is in this world, mine is not. That is why I told you that you would die in your sins. If you do not believe that I am what I am, you will die in your sins.' 25 They asked him, 'Who are you?' Jesus answered, 'Why 26 should I speak to you at all? I have much to say about you—and in judgement. But he who sent me speaks the truth, and what I heard from him I report to the world.' 27 They did not understand that he was speaking to them 28 about the Father. So Jesus said to them, 'When you have lifted up the Son of Man you will know that I am what I am. I do nothing on my own authority, but in all that 29 I say, I have been taught by my Father. He who sent me is present with me, and has not left me alone; for I 30 always do what is acceptable to him.' As he said this, many put their faith in him.

✻ Jesus declares that he is going where the Jews cannot follow and that, unable to find him as Saviour, they will perish unredeemed. They think he is planning suicide. It was a misconception not without its truth, for he was indeed voluntarily 'laying down his life' (10: 18)—helped out by the Jews. They cannot follow him (Jesus says) because their origin and outlook belong to a quite different world from him, and only doom awaits them unless they believe that he is the Eternal One. Puzzled by this language, they ask, *Who are you?* Sadly Jesus replies, 'What I have been telling you all along. And if I have many hard judgements to make on you, I have no alternative, because my Sender is the truth, and I am simply here to say what he bids me.'

Then, as they miss his meaning, Jesus hints at a time of coming revelation. When the Jews stand below the cross on which they have put him, the truth about his person will begin to dawn on them (cf. Mark 14: 62). Meantime, in all he says and does he is the obedient pupil of a Father who never forsakes him.

This simple claim to divine companionship, adds John, moved many to adherence.

24. *I am what I am.* A formula found four times in the Gospel (8: 24, 28, 58 and 13: 19), and probably complete in itself. Its roots are in such Old Testament passages as Exod. 3: 14; Deut. 32: 39 and Isa. 43: 10. In Greek there are only two words: 'I am', and they have the timelessness of God. 'Am' expresses the eternal being of Christ, setting him on a level with God. The N.E.B.'s *I am what I am*, with its echo of God's word to Moses in Exod. 3: 14, is an excellent attempt at translation.

25. *Why should I speak to you at all?* This possible, but not very suitable, rendering expresses an impatient 'What is the good of further talk?' The alternative rendering, given in the N.E.B.'s footnote, makes better sense: 'What I have been telling you all along.'

28. *lifted up.* The verb carries the double meaning of (*a*) put on the cross; and (*b*) exalt to glory. Here it is a grim suggestion that the Jews will help him on his upward way—by killing him. *

THE CLIMAX OF THE CONTROVERSY

31 Turning to the Jews who had believed him, Jesus said, 'If you dwell within the revelation I have brought, you are
32 indeed my disciples; you shall know the truth, and the
33 truth will set you free.' They replied, 'We are Abraham's descendants; we have never been in slavery to any man. What do you mean by saying, "You will become free
34 men"?' 'In very truth I tell you', said Jesus, 'that everyone
35 who commits sin is a slave. The slave has no permanent standing in the household, but the son belongs to it for
36 ever. If then the Son sets you free, you will indeed be free.
37 'I know that you are descended from Abraham, but you are bent on killing me because my teaching makes no
38 headway with you. I am revealing in words what I saw in my Father's presence; and you are revealing in action
39 what you learned from your father.' They retorted, 'Abraham is our father.' 'If you were Abraham's chil-
40 dren', Jesus replied, 'you would do as Abraham did. As it is, you are bent on killing me, a man who told you the truth, as I heard it from God. That is not how Abraham
41 acted. You are doing your own father's work.'

They said, 'We are not base-born; God is our father,
42 and God alone.' Jesus said, 'If God were your father, you would love me, for God is the source of my being, and from him I come. I have not come of my own accord; he
43 sent me. Why do you not understand my language? It is because my revelation is beyond your grasp.

44 'Your father is the devil and you choose to carry out your father's desires. He was a murderer from the beginning, and is not rooted in the truth; there is no truth

in him. When he tells a lie he is speaking his own language, for he is a liar and the father of lies. But I speak the truth 45 and therefore you do not believe me. Which of you can 46 prove me in the wrong? If what I say is true, why do you not believe me? He who has God for his father 47 listens to the words of God. You are not God's children; that is why you do not listen.'

The Jews answered, 'Are we not right in saying that 48 you are a Samaritan, and that you are possessed?' 'I am 49 not possessed,' said Jesus; 'the truth is that I am honouring my Father, but you dishonour me. I do not care about 50 my own glory; there is one who does care, and he is judge. In very truth I tell you, if anyone obeys my 51 teaching he shall never know what it is to die.'

The Jews said, 'Now we are certain that you are 52 possessed. Abraham is dead; the prophets are dead; and yet you say, "If anyone obeys my teaching he shall not know what it is to die." Are you greater than our father 53 Abraham, who is dead? The prophets are dead too. What do you claim to be?'

Jesus replied, 'If I glorify myself, that glory of mine is 54 worthless. It is the Father who glorifies me, he of whom you say, "He is our God", though you do not know him. 55 But I know him; if I said that I did not know him I should be a liar like you. But in truth I know him and obey his word.

'Your father Abraham was overjoyed to see my day; 56 he saw it and was glad.' The Jews protested, 'You are not 57 yet fifty years old. How can you have seen Abraham?' Jesus said, 'In very truth I tell you, before Abraham was 58 born, I am.'

59 They picked up stones to throw at him, but Jesus was
not to be seen; and he left the temple.

✻ In this section Jesus has hard words to say about the
Jews. Can the 'gentle Jesus' have so expressed himself? Before we answer, we should bear three points in mind:

(1) The judgement here pronounced on the Jews is not
severer than that in Matt. 23: 13-39. Jesus could be very
'ungentle' in his condemnation of evil.

(2) Since this Gospel is the interpretation of a memory, the
relations between Jesus and the Jews which climaxed in their
rejection of him are here, in retrospect, seen as possessing this
hardness from the outset.

(3) Probably the later hostility between Church and synagogue has darkened the record.

Now let us summarize the to-and-fro of the argument.

Jesus begins by offering freedom to all 'believing Jews' who
will steadfastly follow him. They reply that they have never
been slaves: why then this talk of becoming 'free'? The
answer is that men, politically free, may be—indeed are—
slaves of sin; but true freedom may be theirs through the gift of
him who is the rightful Son in his Father's house (verses 31-6).

The Jews had called themselves 'Abraham's descendants'.
Jesus declares that, if they really were such, they would morally
resemble that famous 'friend of God'. But in trying to kill an
innocent man for uttering God-given truth they show how
unlike Abraham they are. They must have some other father
(verses 37-41).

They answer, hotly, that they are not bastards but true
children of God. Jesus retorts that, if they really were, they
would be welcoming him as God's messenger to men (which
clearly they are not doing). They have failed to grasp his
revelation, the Word in his words. In short, their father is the
devil; and this is why they wish to kill him, preferring lies to
truth (verses 42-7).

The Jews reply that his mind is deranged. Denying this,

Jesus allows that he is certainly unusual in caring for God's glory, not his own. (In an aside: there is One who does care for it—God the Judge.) Then, suddenly, he offers eternal life to all who will obey him (verses 48–51).

This, for the Jews, is the final proof of his madness. This braggart is claiming to be greater than Abraham and the prophets who were all mortal. Does he rank himself above them? Jesus replies that he is no braggart but that he does know God as they do not. Indeed he is that person (the Messiah) whose day Abraham was allowed to see in vision. When the Jews reply that a man under fifty cannot possibly have seen Abraham, Jesus makes the majestic claim, *before Abraham was born, I am*. Whereas Abraham, like any other mortal man, came into existence, Jesus is beyond and above time (verses 52–8).

When they attempt to stone him for blasphemy, Jesus is not to be found.

The breach with Jewry has come. We shall see it maturing in the episodes that follow. It will climax in a crucifixion.

31. True freedom is a filial relation with God which he offers men through his Son, the liberator from the slavery of sin. Paul taught the same truth.

33. *we have never been in slavery*. Had they forgotten the Babylonian captivity? Or the bondage in Egypt?

38. Jesus' contrast between *my Father* and *your father* makes the Jews (rightly) suspect something sinister.

39. *you would do as Abraham did*, i.e. welcome heavenly guests (Gen. 18: 1 ff.)

41. *We are not base-born*. Perhaps a malicious reference to Jesus' supposed illegitimacy. This slander was to become common in Jewish circles later.

43. The Jews cannot discern the *logos* (revelation) in his *lalia* (language)—the Word (of God) in his words.

44. *He was a murderer from the beginning*. Cf. 1 John 3: 8. Why? Because he robbed Adam of his immortality. The reference is to the story of the Fall (Gen. 2: 17; 3: 19).

48. *you are a Samaritan*, i.e. a half-breed heretic.

51 f. The Jews suppose that Jesus is promising immunity from physical death. Abraham and the prophets, they say, kept God's word, but they died. Do you expect us to believe you are greater than they?

56. According to rabbinical tradition, Abraham was allowed to see the future history of Israel, including the Messianic Age (cf. 2 Esdras 3: 14). May we not take Jesus' words *Abraham was overjoyed to see my day* to mean that in him was the vindication of Abraham's faith? Without Christ, Abraham's faith is a question without an answer.

58. In Christ's claim the contrast is between an existence begun by birth and an absolute existence. Cf. Ps. 90: 2

Before the mountains were brought forth...
Even from everlasting to everlasting, THOU ART.... ✶

CURE OF A MAN BORN BLIND

9 As he went on his way Jesus saw a man blind from his
2 birth. His disciples put the question, 'Rabbi, who sinned,
3 this man or his parents? Why was he born blind?' 'It is not that this man or his parents sinned,' Jesus answered; 'he was born blind that God's power might be displayed
4 in curing him. While daylight lasts we must carry on the work of him who sent me; night comes, when no one can
5 work. While I am in the world I am the light of the world.'
6 With these words he spat on the ground and made a
7 paste with the spittle; he spread it on the man's eyes, and said to him, 'Go and wash in the pool of Siloam.' (The name means 'sent'.) The man went away and washed, and when he returned he could see.
8 His neighbours and those who were accustomed to see him begging said, 'Is not this the man who used to sit

and beg?' Others said, 'Yes, this is the man.' Others 9
again said, 'No, but it is someone like him.' The man
himself said, 'I am the man.' They asked him, 'How were 10
your eyes opened?' He replied, 'The man called Jesus 11
made a paste and smeared my eyes with it, and told me
to go to Siloam and wash. I went and washed, and
gained my sight.' 'Where is he?' they asked. He 12
answered, 'I do not know.'

✻ The tense controversy of chapter 8 now makes way for one
of the Gospel's most vivid narratives. At 8: 12 Jesus had
declared himself the light of the world. This truth is now
shown by his restoration of sight to a man born blind.
According to Old Testament prophecy, such giving of sight
was to be a mark of the Messianic time—'Then the eyes of the
blind shall be opened' (Isa. 35: 5). The blind man's cure however is a dramatic symbol of the Christ who gives light to
those in spiritual darkness.

1. *As he went on his way*: presumably along a road from the
Temple on the festival's last day.

2. *who sinned?* The disciples assume a necessary connexion
between sin and suffering, as did many Jews, despite the
passionate protest of Job. Even a congenital defect like this
one represented a divine punishment of sin. When was the sin
committed? There were three possibilities: in the womb, in
some previous existence, or by the parents.

3. But, as in Luke 13: 1–5, Jesus denies the connexion. The
vital question is not, Who is responsible? but, How may this
tragic fact be turned to the glory of God? Let Christians take
note. Their primary duty is not to torture their minds over the
mystery of evil but, with God's help, to do what they can to
remove it.

4. *daylight...night*. One for work, the other for rest. Jesus
must press on with his Father's work of salvation while the
light lasts. *we*: Jesus associates the disciples with himself.

5. Cf. 8: 12.

6. Sabbath law forbade the anointing of eyes and the making of clay. Here is another illustration of 5: 17. Christ like his Father never ceases, even on the Sabbath, to give life. Spittle was, and is still, commonly supposed in the East to have curative virtue. Thus we read in Doughty's *Arabia Deserta*: 'A young mother, yet a tender girl, brought her babe and bade me spit on the child's sore eyes; this ancient Semitic custom I afterwards found wherever I came in Arabia.' Cf. also Mark 8: 23.

7. *Go and wash in the pool of Siloam*: at the south of the Temple area. The pool was named in Hebrew 'sent' because its waters were 'sent' (conducted) by aqueduct. But since John likes to call Christ the One 'sent' by God (eighteen times in all), he is probably thinking of him as 'the spiritual Siloam' (just as Paul called him the rock in the wilderness, 1 Cor. 10: 4).

8. The man had been a beggar, presumably at one of the Temple gates, like the one who accosted Peter and John (Acts 3: 2).

11. *The man called Jesus.* This is the first step in the man's growing grasp of Jesus' true spiritual stature. Six verses later Jesus is for him *a prophet.* Later (verse 33) he is *a man come from God.* Finally (verses 35 ff.) he is the Messiah demanding his homage. In this way, many ascend gradually to belief in Christ's divinity. If to begin with he is 'the finest man who ever lived', in the end he is 'My Lord and my God'. ✵

THE REACTION

13 The man who had been blind was brought before the
14 Pharisees. As it was a Sabbath day when Jesus made the
15 paste and opened his eyes, the Pharisees now asked him
by what means he had gained his sight. The man told
them, 'He spread a paste on my eyes; then I washed, and
16 now I can see.' Some of the Pharisees said, 'This fellow is

no man of God; he does not keep the Sabbath.' Others said, 'How could such signs come from a sinful man?' So they took different sides.

Then they continued to question him: 'What have you 17 to say about him? It was your eyes he opened.' He answered, 'He is a prophet.' The Jews would not believe 18 that the man had been blind and had gained his sight, until they had summoned his parents and questioned 19 them: 'Is this man your son? Do you say that he was born blind? How is it that he can see now?' The parents 20 replied, 'We know that he is our son, and that he was born blind. But how it is that he can now see, or who 21 opened his eyes, we do not know. Ask him; he is of age; he will speak for himself.' His parents gave this answer 22 because they were afraid of the Jews; for the Jewish authorities had already agreed that anyone who acknowledged Jesus as Messiah should be banned from the synagogue. That is why the parents said, 'He is of age; 23 ask him.'

So for the second time they summoned the man who 24 had been blind, and said, 'Speak the truth before God. We know that this fellow is a sinner.' 'Whether or not he 25 is a sinner, I do not know', the man replied. 'All I know is this: once I was blind, now I can see.' 'What did he do 26 to you?' they asked. 'How did he open your eyes?' 'I 27 have told you already,' he retorted, 'but you took no notice. Why do you want to hear it again? Do you also want to become his disciples?' Then they became abusive. 28 'You are that man's disciple,' they said, 'but we are disciples of Moses. We know that God spoke to Moses, but 29 as for this fellow, we do not know where he comes from.'

30   The man replied, 'What an extraordinary thing! Here is a man who has opened my eyes, yet you do not know

31 where he comes from! It is common knowledge that God does not listen to sinners; he listens to anyone who

32 is devout and obeys his will. To open the eyes of a man

33 born blind—it is unheard of since time began. If that man had not come from God he could have done nothing.'

34 'Who are you to give us lessons,' they retorted, 'born and bred in sin as you are?' Then they expelled him from the synagogue.

✳ The reaction to the miracle falls into three parts: (1) examination of the blind man; (2) examination of his parents; and (3) second examination and expulsion.

The result of the first hearing by the Pharisees (verses 13-17) is a 'split' in their ranks; for some, Christ's treatment of the Sabbath is enough to brand him as a godless fellow; for others, the idea of a godless miracle-worker is a contradiction in terms. On the evidence of his cure the blind man is ready to pronounce him *a prophet*.

Appeal is next made (verses 18-23) to the man's parents in order to reach a finding. They identify their son and do not deny the cure. But, unwilling to involve themselves further, they refer the Pharisees to the son himself: *Ask him; he is of age*, i.e. he is a legal witness. Their caution, John explains, sprang from a fear that anyone who confessed Jesus' Messiahship would be *banned from the synagogue*—cut off from the fellowship of Israel. Temporary, not permanent, exclusion is probably meant.

So the Pharisees call the man for a second hearing (verses 24-34). First they put him on oath: *Speak the truth before God*. The Greek means literally 'Give glory to God'. But a glance at Joshua 7: 19 shows that this really means 'Make a frank confession', for these are the words Joshua uses when urging Achan to confess his theft. The man, refusing to 'get mixed up in theology', replies, *All I know is this: once I was blind, now I can see.* An ounce of real experience is worth a pound of rabbinical theology. (Intellectual problems about Christ's person do not need to be solved before men can receive his benefits.) The man now grows bolder: does their request to hear his story again, he says sarcastically, mean that they want to become Jesus' disciples? At this they staunchly avow themselves disciples of Moses and become abusive. *We know that God spoke to Moses, but as for this fellow, we do not know where he comes from.* Then the man really warms to attack: 'How very odd that you, whose business it is to know all about miracle-workers, should not see the truth about him—and yet he opened my eyes. Why, everybody knows that God does not favour sinners but only those who obey him. Anyone who could work such an unparalleled miracle as this must have God at his back.' No wonder they descend to personalities: *Who are you to give us lessons,* they say, *born and bred in sin as you are?* And they expel him from the synagogue. ✳

THE SEQUEL

Jesus heard that they had expelled him. When he found 35
him he asked, 'Have you faith in the Son of Man?' The 36
man answered, 'Tell me who he is, sir, that I should put
my faith in him.' 'You have seen him,' said Jesus; 'indeed, 37
it is he who is speaking to you.' 'Lord, I believe', he said, 38
and bowed before him.

Jesus said, 'It is for judgement that I have come into 39
this world—to give sight to the sightless and to make
blind those who see.' Some Pharisees in his company 40
asked, 'Do you mean that we are blind?' 'If you were 41
blind,' said Jesus, 'you would not be guilty, but because
you say "We see", your guilt remains.

✻ 'The Jews cast him out of the Temple,' said Chrysostom, 'the Lord of the Temple found him.' *Have you faith in the Son of Man?* (there is a less good reading, *Son of God*) must be a veiled way of asking 'Do you believe in the Messiah?' When the man asks only to know him that he may believe in him, Jesus reveals his identity as he had done to the Samaritan woman, and receives his homage. So the blind man who has passed from Judaism to Christianity passes out of the story as the typical believer.

The concluding verses (39–41) draw out the meaning of Jesus' presence in our world. Though judgement was not the primary purpose of his coming (3: 17), it was the inevitable result. The man's recovery of his sight is typical of what is going on in the realm of spiritual enlightenment. The eyes of the unlearned are opened; the supposedly 'enlightened', by refusing to obey, have blinded themselves. Are the Pharisees blind? They expect to be told that they are. They are told that their blindness would be an excuse; it is their claim to sight that condemns them.

As sheer drama, comments C. H. Dodd, this 'is one of the most brilliant passages in the Gospel, rich in the tragic irony of which the evangelist is master. The one-time blind beggar stands before his betters, to be badgered into denying the one thing of which he is certain. But the defendant proper is Jesus himself, judged *in absentia*. In some sort, the man whom Christ enlightens pleads the cause of light. When he is cast out, it is Christ whom the judges have rejected. Then comes the dramatic *peripeteia* (reversal). Jesus swiftly turns the tables on his judges and pronounces sentence.' ✻

THE GOOD SHEPHERD AND HIS FLOCK

10 'In truth I tell you, in very truth, the man who does not enter the sheepfold by the door, but climbs in some other 2 way, is nothing but a thief or a robber. The man who enters by the door is the shepherd in charge of the sheep. The door-keeper admits him, and the sheep hear his 3 voice; he calls his own sheep by name, and leads them out. When he has brought them all out, he goes ahead 4 and the sheep follow, because they know his voice. They 5 will not follow a stranger; they will run away from him, because they do not recognize the voice of strangers.'

This was a parable that Jesus told them, but they did not 6 understand what he meant by it.

✻ Judgement was the theme with which chapter 9 ended, and the link with what now follows. Its core is a long allegorical parable in which Jesus indicts the Pharisees as unworthy rulers of Israel. The key to it is in Ezekiel's famous 34th chapter. There Israel's rulers are arraigned as false shepherds; and, in prophetic vision, God deposes them, seeks out his lost sheep, sets over them a shepherd Messiah of David's line, and delivers his flock from all evil.

So in John 10 the Pharisees are accused of being hireling and heartless shepherds, and the veiled claim is made that in Christ's mission God's promise of deliverance is fulfilled. The shepherd of Ezekiel's vision has become incarnate in One who truly cares for God's sheep and who by his life-giving death brings them deliverance.

The parable itself (verses 1–5) tells of a shepherd whose every act reveals him to be a true one, and no interloper. He enters by the fold door (not over the wall), and his voice is familiar. He calls the sheep by their individual names. He leads them out to pasture and the sheep willingly follow him, though they react quite differently to strangers.

If we remember that 'Shepherd' was one of Messiah's names, and put the story back into John's own phrases, the meaning becomes clear. There is but one deliverer who comes to *his own* (1: 11), and calls them to *follow* him (1: 44). They *hear his voice* (5: 25), and he calls them by their own names

(11: 43). Those who follow him do 'not walk in the dark' but have the 'light of life' (8: 12). It is a pastoral picture of God's true Messiah.

But the Pharisees failed to see that the parable was told for their rebuking.

1. *the sheepfold* is a courtyard in front of the house where the sheep are brought in for the night. A single door in the courtyard wall, guarded by a porter, admits to both house and sheep. The true shepherd enters by the door, with the porter's permission. Thieves must climb the wall.

4. *he goes ahead*: as an eastern shepherd always does. *

CHRIST THE DOOR

7 So Jesus spoke again: 'In truth, in very truth I tell you, I
8 am the door of the sheepfold. The sheep paid no heed to any who came before me, for these were all thieves and
9 robbers. I am the door; anyone who comes into the fold through me shall be safe. He shall go in and out and shall find pasturage.

10 'The thief comes only to steal, to kill, to destroy; I have come that men may have life, and may have it in all its fullness.'

* The first application of the parable. Jesus is the door of the fold. It is by this door alone that men enter the fold (the new Israel, of which the disciples form the nucleus). If they come in trusting in Jesus, they will find safety, freedom, sustenance. (In plain terms, salvation is by faith in Christ alone and membership of his Church.)

But what is meant by the harsh-sounding reference to *thieves and robbers* who came before Christ? The allusion is not to the Old Testament prophets but to Israel's false rulers and deliverers. It is a strong declaration, couched in negative terms, that all truth is now present in the incarnate Lord.

There follows (verse 10) one of the Gospel's great sayings: *life...in all its fullness*, life that is life indeed, life lived in the presence of God, life with the quality of eternity about it—this Jesus came to bestow on men. But, as he will make clear, the gift of such life can only come through his death. Here is the supreme paradox of the Gospel. The life of the Christian community depends upon the death of Jesus. ✳

CHRIST THE SHEPHERD

'I am the good shepherd; the good shepherd lays down 11 his life for the sheep. The hireling, when he sees the 12 wolf coming, abandons the sheep and runs away, because he is no shepherd and the sheep are not his. Then the wolf harries the flock and scatters the sheep. The man runs away 13 because he is a hireling and cares nothing for the sheep.

'I am the good shepherd; I know my own sheep and 14 my sheep know me—as the Father knows me and I know 15 the Father—and I lay down my life for the sheep. But 16 there are other sheep of mine, not belonging to this fold, whom I must bring in; and they too will listen to my voice. There will then be one flock, one shepherd. The 17 Father loves me because I lay down my life, to receive it back again. No one has robbed me of it; I am laying it 18 down of my own free will. I have the right to lay it down, and I have the right to receive it back again; this charge I have received from my Father.'

These words once again caused a split among the 19 Jews. Many of them said, 'He is possessed, he is raving. 20 Why listen to him?' Others said, 'No one possessed by 21 an evil spirit could speak like this. Could an evil spirit open blind men's eyes?'

✲ Now follows the second application of the parable. 'When he brings us to the Father,' said Chrysostom, 'he calls himself a Door; when he takes care of us, a Shepherd.'

I am the good shepherd. The Greek word for *good* implies beauty as well as fitness for the task. Jesus' fitness for the work his Father has given him is shown by his readiness to die for his flock. His opposite is the *hireling* whose only interest in the sheep is his wages and who abandons them at the threat of danger.

Then, as Jesus compares the mutual understanding between himself and his flock to that between the Father and himself, and reaffirms his devotion unto death for them, he looks beyond the fold of Judaism to the wider world and sees *other sheep* of his waiting to be gathered in. He is thinking of his mission to the Gentiles after he is 'glorified'. When that vision is fully realized, *there will then be one flock, one shepherd.*

The discourse climaxes in the prophecy of his death and resurrection (verses 17 f.). The death in prospect for him is due, he says, not to circumstances but to his *own free will. I have the right to lay it down.* Yet, paradoxically, this self-determination to die and rise again is a *charge* he has received from his Father. The Son's freedom therefore consists in spontaneously obeying his Father's commandment.

The result of this discourse was again a divided opinion among his hearers. Some reverted to the theory of demon-possession; others replied that both his words and deeds made nonsense of such a theory.

12. *The hireling.* The contrast is between a truly devoted shepherd and one who is interested only in the money his work brings.

15. *the Father knows me and I know the Father.* This is the same claim as is made by Jesus in Matt. 11:27. The idea that the same mutual understanding exists between Jesus and his disciples as exists between him and his Father is one to be developed in the Farewell Discourses.

16. Can Jesus really have cherished the great vision con-

tained in the words *one flock, one shepherd*? Why not? Ezekiel spoke of one supreme shepherd of God's flock (Ezek. 34: 23); Isaiah envisaged the Lord's Servant becoming 'a light of the Gentiles' (Isa. 42: 6); and Jesus predicted a time when men would come from all the corners of the earth to sit down in the kingdom of God (Matt. 8: 11).

17. Notice the two verbs which Jesus uses for his death and resurrection: 'lay down' and 'take' (again). They provide a clue to the understanding of the foot-washing in John 13.

18. *No one has robbed me of it.* The crucifixion lies in the future, but Jesus views his death as if it were a past event. Cf. 16: 33. ✳

THE FEAST OF DEDICATION

It was winter, and the festival of the Dedication was being 22 held in Jerusalem. Jesus was walking in the temple 23 precincts, in Solomon's Cloister. The Jews gathered round 24 him and asked: 'How long must you keep us in suspense? If you are the Messiah say so plainly.' 'I have told you,' 25 said Jesus, 'but you do not believe. My deeds done in my Father's name are my credentials, but because you are 26 not sheep of my flock you do not believe. My own sheep 27 listen to my voice; I know them and they follow me. I 28 give them eternal life and they shall never perish; no one shall snatch them from my care. My Father who has 29 given them to me is greater than all, and no one can snatch them out of the Father's care. My Father and I are 30 one.'

Once again the Jews picked up stones to stone him. At 31,32 this Jesus said to them, 'I have set before you many good deeds, done by my Father's power; for which of these would you stone me?' The Jews replied, 'We are not 33 going to stone you for any good deed, but for your

34 blasphemy. You, a mere man, claim to be a god.' Jesus answered, 'Is it not written in your own Law, "I said:
35 You are gods"? Those are called gods to whom the word of God was delivered—and Scripture cannot be set aside.
36 Then why do you charge me with blasphemy because I, consecrated and sent into the world by the Father, said, "I am God's son"?

37 'If I am not acting as my Father would, do not believe
38 me. But if I am, accept the evidence of my deeds, even if you do not believe me, so that you may recognize and know that the Father is in me, and I in the Father.'

39 This provoked them to one more attempt to seize him. But he escaped from their clutches.

✻ These verses describe the last direct encounter between Jesus and the Jews during the ministry.

It occurs at the festival of *Dedication* (in Hebrew, *Hanukkah*). This commemorated the rededication of the Temple in 165 B.C. by Judas the Maccabee after its desecration, three years before, by the Seleucid conqueror, Antiochus Epiphanes. Held at the winter solstice (Christmas time), it lasted eight days and was 'the feast of the New Age'.

The season was severe, John tells us, so that Jesus was teaching under shelter *in Solomon's Cloister* on the east side of the Temple area. (Details like these strongly suggest that the evangelist was a Jerusalem Jew.)

Surrounding him, the Jews demand an unambiguous answer to the question of his Messiahship. *How long must you keep us in suspense? If you are the Messiah say so plainly.* No more parables, but a plain yes or no!

Though he had confessed his Messiahship to the Samaritan woman (4: 26), Jesus had never openly claimed it in his conversation with the Jews. How could he? Messiah he was, but his conception of it—witness the temptation story (Matt. 4:

106

1–11; Luke 4: 1–12)—was so utterly different from theirs that a plain yes to their question would have been quite misleading. Nevertheless, all his actions presumed it, and it is to these that he now points them: *My deeds done in my Father's name are my credentials.* His works—those signs in which power is used for love's purposes—are his evidence. (So in the earlier Gospels—see Luke 7: 22 f.—he had replied to a like question from John the Baptist lying in prison.) But, however clear the evidence, the Jews will not hear it, because they are not *sheep of my flock.* (Chrysostom comments: 'If ye follow me not, it is not because I am not a shepherd, but because ye are not my sheep.') Those who are, hear, follow, and are safe for ever. To them Jesus gives *eternal life. They shall never perish,* he says, and *no one shall snatch them from my care.* (So Paul said in Rom. 8: 35 ff. that no power in the world or out of it could sunder Christ's people from God's love pledged to them in Christ.) Why can Jesus so confidently declare that *no one shall snatch them* from his care? Because this is true of the Father, and what is true of him is true also of the Son. For (he adds) *My Father and I are one.* The unity is one of will rather than of substance: 'The Son thinks the Father's thoughts, and wills the Father's purpose, and acts in the Father's power' (T. W. Manson). This claim *was* blasphemy, if it was not true. When the Jews picked up their stones, they showed that they understood this much (verse 31).

But, before they can throw them, Jesus turns their attention from his words to his deeds: *I have set before you many good deeds, done by my Father's power.* They are deeds which, if the Jews could but see it, exhibit the very goodness of his heavenly Father. For which of them, he asks ironically, do they wish to stone him?

The Jews, however, prefer to fasten on his 'blasphemous' saying. Anyone can see that he is a *mere man,* yet he claims to be *a god.* Is not this blasphemy?

Jesus' reply is so typical a piece of Jewish argumentation that it rings with authenticity. He directs them to Ps. 82: 6, and his argument is: If Scripture (which you will not question) calls men commissioned by God to act for him 'gods', one whom the Father has made his consecrated ambassador to the world can hardly be accused of blasphemy for calling himself 'God's son'. If human leaders have been called gods, how much more may one greater than they make a lesser claim— to be not God but God's son.

Yet Jesus is not content to answer them with what, after all, is a play on words. He points again to his deeds: *If I am not acting as my Father would, do not believe me. But if I am, accept the evidence of my deeds, even if you do not believe me, so that you may recognize and know that the Father is in me, and I in the Father.* On the meaning of 'recognize' and 'know', see the note on verse 38. But what is meant by *the Father is in me, and I in the Father*? The Father is in Christ as in the *organ* through which he expresses himself. Christ is in the Father as in the *element* in which he lives and works.

This claim leads to yet another half-hearted attempt to arrest him. His time was not yet come.

23. *Jesus was walking in the temple precincts.* Cf. Mark 11: 27.

29. This is the Christian version of a truth enunciated in the Old Testament. 'I, even I, am the Lord; and beside me there is no saviour...there is none that can deliver out of my hand' (Isa. 43: 11, 13); 'The Lord is my shepherd...though I walk through the valley of the shadow of death, I will fear no evil; for thou art with me' (Ps. 23: 1, 4); 'the souls of the righteous are in the hand of God, and no torment shall touch them' (Wisdom 3: 1).

30. 'Unclouded open-ness of the mind of the Son to the Father—that was the essence of his being—a profound inner sense of harmony and indeed unity of will' (Sanday).

34 f. Jesus implies a kind of belief in the divinity of man in relation to God's purposes. It is very unlikely that an argument like this, which does not clearly set Christ apart from other men, would ever have been devised by an early Christian. Note that the *Law* means here the Old Testament.

36. *consecrated.* Set apart for a holy purpose. Cf. 17: 19.

38. *that you may recognize and know.* Literally, 'that you may know and go on knowing'. A single act of perception is to pass into a permanent state of understanding. The conviction is to be realized again and again. *

Victory over Death

MINISTRY IN PERAEA

J ESUS WITHDREW again across the Jordan, to the place 40
where John had been baptizing earlier. There he stayed, while crowds came to him. They said, 'John gave us no 41 miraculous sign, but all that he said about this man was true.' Many came to believe in him there. 42

* These verses describe a ministry of Jesus east of Jordan, i.e. in Peraea—a ministry also recorded in Mark 10: 1. Jesus, perhaps because of mounting hostility, goes back to the place where the Baptist had baptized and borne his witness to Jesus (1: 28). If the Jerusalem Jews have rejected their Messiah, here in Transjordan humble folk acknowledge the truth of what John had said and confess their faith in Jesus.

This paragraph sums up the ministry to Israel now closing. But it does more. It prefaces the supreme miracle of the raising of Lazarus and sets in train the events in which the Baptist's words will be fulfilled, 'there is the Lamb of God... who takes away the sin of the world'. *

THE RAISING OF LAZARUS

* The story of Lazarus expresses in action the truth of 5: 21: 'As the Father raises the dead and gives them life, so the Son gives life to men.' But this is more than the story of Lazarus

raised to life; it is also, as we shall see, the story of Jesus going to death in order to vanquish death.

Two serious problems arise here. First: did Jesus really raise Lazarus from the dead? To this question we may reply, (1) that Jesus did claim to raise the dead (Luke 7: 22) and that the Synoptics contain two stories of such 'raisings' (the widow of Nain's son and Jairus's daughter); and (2) that, if Jesus is God incarnate (as John and most Christians believe), we cannot say the miracle is incredible.

The other problem is this. Why does not Mark, the earliest Gospel, record an event which, in John's view (11: 53), made the Jewish authorities resolve to kill Jesus? Mark 11: 18, however, tells us that it was the cleansing of the Temple—an event John sets early in his Gospel—which provoked their fatal intervention.

Most scholars, if asked to choose, would prefer Mark's testimony here (though, as Barrett warns us, we ought not to put too much weight on Mark 11: 18). If we prefer to follow John, as some do, we may think up reasons for Mark's silence about Lazarus, as, for example, that the Galilean Peter (whose testimony stands behind Mark) was not present at the raising.

No satisfactory solution of the problem has been found, or perhaps—since we do not know all the facts—ever will be. But in view (*a*) of the vivid and lifelike detail of the narrative, and (*b*) of the abundant evidence that John had access to good independent sources of information about Jesus, the one thing we should not do is to dismiss this famous story as fiction. ✲

NEWS, DELAY, DISSUASION

11 There was a man named Lazarus who had fallen ill. His home was at Bethany, the village of Mary and her sister
2 Martha. (This Mary, whose brother Lazarus had fallen ill, was the woman who anointed the Lord with ointment
3 and wiped his feet with her hair.) The sisters sent a

message to him: 'Sir, you should know that your friend lies ill.' When Jesus heard this he said, 'This sickness will 4 not end in death; it has come for the glory of God, to bring glory to the Son of God.' And therefore, though he 5 loved Martha and her sister and Lazarus, after hearing of his 6 illness Jesus waited for two days in the place where he was.

After this, he said to his disciples, 'Let us go back to 7 Judaea.' 'Rabbi his disciples said, 'it is not long since the 8 Jews there were wanting to stone you. Are you going there again?' Jesus replied, 'Are there not twelve hours 9 of daylight? Anyone can walk in day-time without stumbling, because he sees the light of this world. But if 10 he walks after nightfall he stumbles, because the light fails him.'

After saying this he added, 'Our friend Lazarus has 11 fallen asleep, but I shall go and wake him.' The disciples 12 said, 'Master, if he has fallen asleep he will recover.' Jesus, 13 however, had been speaking of his death, but they thought that he meant natural sleep. Then Jesus spoke out plainly: 14 'Lazarus is dead. I am glad not to have been there; it will 15 be for your good and for the good of your faith. But let us go to him.' Thomas, called 'the Twin', said to his fellow- 16 disciples, 'Let us also go, that we may die with him.'

✻ Lazarus had fallen ill at Bethany where he lived with his two sisters (for the sisters see Luke 10: 38–42). But Luke does not name their village or tell us that they had a brother called Lazarus. Here, in verse 2, John identifies Mary with the woman who anointed Jesus in the house of Simon the Leper (Mark 14: 3–9)—a story John will tell later (12: 1–9), substituting Lazarus for Simon.

When the sisters inform Jesus of their brother's illness, he replies that it *will not end in death*. Death there may be, but it will not be the final issue. The end will be *the glory of God* and the glorification of his Son. How will he be glorified? What he will do for Lazarus will make many believe in him. Yet the evangelist means us to read still more into 'glorified'. Christ's raising of Lazarus will prove—see verses 47 ff.—the cause of his other and greater glorification—on the cross.

Despite his love for the Bethany family, Christ lets two days pass before acting. The explanation of this 'callousness' is that, as in 2: 4 and 7: 6, he obeys his Father's will; and that will is now delay. When at length he proposes a return *to Judaea*, his disciples point out the obvious danger. Jesus answers in a parable (verses 9 f.) which means: 'Your anxiety is premature. My day has not yet run its course.' Superficially, the parable contrasts walking in the sunlight, which is safe, and walking in the dark, which is not: but since Christ is *the light of this world*, the deeper meaning is that he who walks through the world by faith in him is secure against all spiritual accidents.

Our friend Lazarus has fallen asleep, says Jesus (verse 11). *Fall asleep* is a euphemism for death; but the disciples misunderstand it as natural sleep. Such sleep does a sick man good. If Lazarus has won a little natural sleep, his chances of recovery are excellent. So Jesus has to tell them the stark truth. *I am glad not to have been there;* he adds, *it will be for your good and for the good of your faith*. How? The recovery of Lazarus from death would certainly be a more remarkable miracle than his recovery from a sick bed. But, again, more is probably meant. Because Lazarus lived (John will relate) Christ died. And was not that death for their good—and for the world's also?

When Jesus gives the command to go, Thomas, anticipating the worst, is ready to face it along with Jesus. He is a study in loyal despair.

1. *Lazarus* is the Greek form of Eleazar ('God is my help'). The name crops up quite often in inscriptions.

3. *Sir, you should know that your friend lies ill.* 'Enough that

you know. You are not the one to love and to leave' (Augustine).

16. *Thomas* (Hebrew: *Te'om*) was called 'Didymus' in Greek circles. Both Hebrew and Greek mean 'Twin'. This passage together with 14: 5, 20: 24, 29 and 21: 2 show the man—down-to-earth and unmystical, but brave and loyal. *

THE MEETING AND THE MIRACLE

On his arrival Jesus found that Lazarus had already been 17 four days in the tomb. Bethany was just under two miles 18 from Jerusalem, and many of the people had come from 19 the city to Martha and Mary to condole with them on their brother's death. As soon as she heard that Jesus was 20 on his way, Martha went to meet him, while Mary stayed at home.

Martha said to Jesus, 'If you had been here, sir, my 21 brother would not have died. Even now I know that 22 whatever you ask of God, God will grant you.' Jesus 23 said, 'Your brother will rise again.' 'I know that he will 24 rise again', said Martha, 'at the resurrection on the last day.' Jesus said, 'I am the resurrection and I am life. If a 25 man has faith in me, even though he die, he shall come to life; and no one who is alive and has faith shall ever die. 26 Do you believe this?' 'Lord, I do,' she answered; 'I now 27 believe that you are the Messiah, the Son of God who was to come into the world.'

With these words she went to call her sister Mary, and 28 taking her aside, she said, 'The Master is here; he is asking for you.' When Mary heard this she rose up quickly 29 and went to him. Jesus had not yet reached the village, 30 but was still at the place where Martha left him. The 31

Jews who were in the house condoling with Mary, when they saw her start up and leave the house, went after her, for they supposed that she was going to the tomb to weep there.

32 So Mary came to the place where Jesus was. As soon as she caught sight of him she fell at his feet and said, 'O sir, if you had only been here my brother would not have
33 died.' When Jesus saw her weeping and the Jews her companions weeping, he sighed heavily and was deeply
34 moved. 'Where have you laid him?' he asked. They
35,36 replied, 'Come and see, sir.' Jesus wept. The Jews said,
37 'How dearly he must have loved him!' But some of them said, 'Could not this man, who opened the blind man's eyes, have done something to keep Lazarus from dying?'
38 Jesus again sighed deeply; then he went over to the
39 tomb. It was a cave, with a stone placed against it. Jesus said, 'Take away the stone.' Martha, the dead man's sister, said to him, 'Sir, by now there will be a stench;
40 he has been there four days.' Jesus said, 'Did I not tell you
41 that if you have faith you will see the glory of God?' So they removed the stone.

Then Jesus looked upwards and said, 'Father, I thank
42 thee: thou hast heard me. I knew already that thou always hearest me, but I spoke for the sake of the people standing round, that they might believe that thou didst send me.'

43 Then he raised his voice in a great cry: 'Lazarus, come
44 forth.' The dead man came out, his hands and feet swathed in linen bands, his face wrapped in a cloth. Jesus said, 'Loose him; let him go.'

✲ Lazarus had been *four days* in the grave when Jesus arrived in Bethany which was *just under two miles from Jerusalem* (lit. 'fifteen furlongs'). In other words, he was really dead, since a man's spirit was supposed to hover over his body for three days and to depart when the change set in. True to her character (see Luke 10: 40) as one who liked to be 'up and doing', Martha goes out to meet Jesus beyond the village (verse 30). *If you had been here...my brother would not have died*, she says, mingling faith with disappointment. But so firm is her trust in Christ's power with God that she is convinced the delay may yet be made good.

Christ's first word to her sounds like a conventional consolation: 'Remember what our faith teaches about resurrection.' So Martha interprets it. But the last day is far away and small comfort. Christ's next word startles. *I am the resurrection and I am life.* He does not deny the traditional doctrine. He declares that he, in his own person, is the victory over death; he is eternal life; and in him what was a future hope has become a present reality. Soon he will dramatize his word by raising Lazarus. But now he adds: *If a man has faith in me, even though he die* [physically], *he shall come to life.* Why? Because in Christ he has touched the very life of God which is immortal. Moreover, *no one who is alive and has faith* [in me] *shall ever die.* He will of course 'pay the last debt to nature'. But, because of that same saving link with Christ, the physical death he must one day experience loses all reality.

When Jesus asks Martha if she believes this, she assents with a complete confession of his Messiahship.

She then returns to announce Christ's arrival to Mary who is still sitting at home, surrounded by comforters. Mary, followed by the Jews, goes out to meet Jesus and throws herself at his feet with the same words as Martha had used, but with tears. The tears move Jesus to take on himself her distress: he *sighed heavily and was deeply moved*—clear proof that Christ's miracles were not done without cost to himself (cf. Mark 5: 30). At his own request, he is taken to the place of the dead; and the sight makes him burst into tears. Some of the bystanders take his tears to be sincere; but others cynically observe that the miracle-worker might have used his powers to save his friend.

The tomb was not a pit with a stone to serve as lid but a hollowed rock with an aperture facing the viewer and a stone at its entrance to keep out wild beasts. When Jesus orders the stone to be removed, Martha dreads the disclosure of her brother's decaying body. Jesus reminds her (and the reader), that only the believer can and will see the glory of God. (*Glory* here, as in Rom. 6: 4, means 'majestic power'.)

Then Jesus looked upwards and said, 'Father, I thank thee: thou hast heard me'. Simple words of thanksgiving as if Lazarus were already restored. But his next words are not so simple: *I knew already that thou always hearest me; but I spoke for the sake of the people standing round, that they might believe that thou didst send me*. The point is not that Jesus did not need to ask for divine power, but that he actually spoke the words aloud so that all might know the true source of his power.

The word of power is now uttered in a loud voice and uses Lazarus's own name (cf. John 10: 3). And *the dead man came out, his hands and feet swathed in linen bands, his face wrapped in a cloth*. Lazarus had been partially bandaged, just as later Christ was to be (19: 40; 20: 5, 7); but, while Jesus left the grave-clothes without human help, Lazarus has to be liberated at Christ's command.

33. *sighed heavily*. Perhaps better: 'was indignant', i.e. at the unbelief of the Jews. ✻

THE REPERCUSSIONS

45 Now many of the Jews who had come to visit Mary and
46 had seen what Jesus did, put their faith in him. But some of them went off to the Pharisees and reported what he had done.

47 Thereupon the chief priests and the Pharisees convened

a meeting of the Council. 'What action are we taking?' they said. 'This man is performing many signs. If we 48 leave him alone like this the whole populace will believe in him. Then the Romans will come and sweep away our temple and our nation.' But one of them, Caiaphas, who 49 was High Priest that year, said, 'You know nothing whatever; you do not use your judgement; it is more to your 50 interest that one man should die for the people, than that the whole nation should be destroyed.' He did not say 51 this of his own accord, but as the High Priest in office that year, he was prophesying that Jesus would die for the nation—die not for the nation alone but to gather to- 52 gether the scattered children of God. So from that day 53 on they plotted his death.

Accordingly Jesus no longer went about publicly in 54 Judaea, but left that region for the country bordering on the desert, and came to a town called Ephraim, where he stayed with his disciples.

The Jewish Passover was now at hand, and many people 55 went up from the country to Jerusalem to purify themselves before the festival. They looked out for Jesus, and 56 as they stood in the temple they asked one another, 'What do you think? Perhaps he is not coming to the festival.' Now the chief priests and the Pharisees had given orders 57 that anyone who knew where he was should give information, so that they might arrest him.

* By raising Lazarus Jesus has signed his death warrant. Henceforward the shadow of the cross lengthens across the story.

Many Jews who had seen the miracle *put their faith* in Jesus, i.e. accepted him as Messiah as they understood the title. But others hurried off to tell the Pharisees; and when they and the chief priests had called a meeting of the Sanhedrin, it was resolved that their further inaction could mean only one thing —a Messianic uprising which would bring in the Roman armies and end in the destruction of both their nation and temple.

At this juncture the High Priest put the issue to the Council with brutal clarity: 'Better a single life should be sacrificed on behalf of God's people than that the whole nation should be doomed to ruin.' This has been called 'the unconscious prophecy'. Consciously, Caiaphas was expressing a piece of cynical expediency; unconsciously, he was summing up the Gospel—see John 3: 16.

The evangelist (verse 51) explains that Caiaphas was speaking more truly than he knew. The High Priest was supposed to have the power of divination; and here we find him unwittingly prophesying that by the death of Jesus the chosen people would become the universal Church.

There was now only one thing for it—Jesus must die (verse 53). Knowing what was afoot, Jesus retired with his disciples to the deserted hill country fifteen miles north-east of Jerusalem. The *town called Ephraim*, now known as Et-Taiyibeh, lies on the road from Samaria to Jericho.

Meanwhile, as the Passover was approaching, pilgrims began to move into Jerusalem for the preliminary ritual purifications. All were agog with excitement. The question was whether Jesus would dare to set foot in the city now that the Jewish authorities had ordered that anyone who knew his whereabouts should reveal it.

49. *Caiaphas, who was High Priest that year.* We must not infer that John supposed the High-Priesthood to be a yearly office. The High Priest held office for life—unless deposed by the Romans, as he often was. Caiaphas in fact held office from A.D. 18 to A.D. 36. John's phrase means 'High Priest in that year of all years'.

52. *the scattered children of God.* Not Jews but Gentiles. Only

by the Shepherd's death can God's scattered sheep be gathered into 'one flock' (10: 16). In the next chapter (12: 24, 32) we shall learn that Jesus' death is necessary in order to 'universalize' his mission. *

THE ANOINTING AT BETHANY

Six days before the Passover festival Jesus came to **12** Bethany, where Lazarus lived whom he had raised from the dead. There a supper was given in his honour, at 2 which Martha served, and Lazarus sat among the guests with Jesus. Then Mary brought a pound of very costly 3 perfume, oil of pure nard, and anointed the feet of Jesus and wiped them with her hair, till the house was filled with the fragrance. At this, Judas Iscariot, a disciple of his 4 —the one who was to betray him—said, 'Why was this 5 perfume not sold for thirty pounds and given to the poor?' He said this, not out of any care for the poor, but 6 because he was a thief; he used to pilfer the money put into the common purse, which was in his charge. 'Leave 7 her alone', said Jesus. 'Let her keep it till the day when she prepares for my burial; for you have the poor among 8 you always, but you will not always have me.'

A great number of the Jews heard that he was there, 9 and came not only to see Jesus but also Lazarus whom he had raised from the dead. The chief priests then resolved 10 to do away with Lazarus as well, since on his account 11 many Jews were going over to Jesus and putting their faith in him.

* Chapter 12 serves as a postscript to the story of Lazarus and as a prelude to that of the Passion.

On the Saturday before Palm Sunday (as we would say)

there was a supper in Jesus' honour in Bethany at which Martha acted as waitress and Lazarus figured among the guests. At it Mary anointed Jesus' feet with some expensive perfume before drying them with her hair, so that the fragrance filled the house. Judas, allegedly concerned for the poor, protested at the extravagance. In fact, comments the evangelist, he was a thief and not above 'raiding' the disciples' *common purse* which he carried. Jesus leapt to Mary's defence. She had anticipated his death by an act of inspired devotion.

What is the relation of this story to those in the earlier gospels (1) of the harlot who anointed Jesus' feet in Simon the Pharisee's house (Luke 7), and (2) of the woman who anointed Jesus' head in Simon the Leper's house in Bethany two days before the Passover (Mark 14)? The story of the harlot surely describes a quite different event; but Mark and John are obviously referring to the same anointing. Why then does John, while apparently basing himself on Mark, make such drastic changes? When we find him evidently borrowing three of Mark's phrases (*pure nard, thirty pounds, Leave her alone*), our first impulse is to say: 'Here is proof positive that John knew and used Mark.' But a study of the differences gives us pause. In Mark the supper comes *after* the triumphal entry; in John *before* it. In Mark the anointer is an *unnamed woman*; in John it is *Mary*. In Mark it is Jesus' *head* which is anointed; in John, *his feet*. When we compare all the facts, it seems likelier that John got his story from the oral tradition than that he borrowed some phrases from Mark and Luke.

Why did Mary do what she did? Obviously her act was an expression of supreme devotion to Jesus. In Mark the woman, when she anoints Jesus (as the Messiah), seems to link his Messiahship with his death. The meaning of John's account is basically the same. Why, Judas had asked, did not Mary sell the perfume and give the *thirty pounds* to the poor? 'It was,' answers Jesus, 'that she might keep it for my burial.' Knowing that Jesus had to die and that his 'hour' had now come, she anticipated his burial by a deed of inspired devotion.

Why did she anoint his *feet*? Perhaps John 13: 10 supplies the clue. There Jesus implies that his washing of the disciples' feet was in fact a complete cleansing. So it is now at Bethany. Mary's act is a symbolical embalming of his whole body for burial, as though he were already dead. And she gives the final proof of her devotion by using her hair—a woman's 'glory' (Paul), to complete her action.

1. *Six days before the Passover*. According to John (13: 1, 18: 28, 19: 31, 42) the Passover began on the Friday evening. Six days before this brings us to the preceding Saturday evening. Cf. Mark 14: 1.

3. *pure* is the best guess at the meaning of the rare Greek word *pistikos*. *Nard* was an oriental ointment.

4. *Judas*. Mark does not name the grumblers.

5. *thirty pounds*. Literally, '300 denarii'. A day-labourer's wage for a whole year.

6. *pilfer* renders the Greek *bastazein* which has the same two meanings as the English 'lift'. Judas carried *the common purse* (lit. 'money-box'), and 'lifted' what was put into it.

7. The meaning of this verse, which is difficult in the Greek, is not certain. The N.E.B. adds the words *when she prepares*, which are not in the original. *It* must then mean 'the rest of the perfume'. But it is easier to suppose that it had all been used. So the marginal reading of the R.V. is to be preferred: 'It was that she might keep it for the day of my burying', i.e. she had kept it just for this special purpose, the death and burial being close at hand.

8. This verse, *for you have the poor among you always, but you will not always have me*, not read by two of our best manuscripts (as the N.E.B. footnote observes), was probably added by a copyist to harmonize it with Matt. 26: 11.

9 ff. Reactions to the raising of Lazarus. Jesus' doom was now sealed. The rulers, many of whom were Sadducees, planned to kill Lazarus as well. Was he not a living refutation of their disbelief in the resurrection? ✳

THE TRIUMPHAL ENTRY

12 The next day the great body of pilgrims who had come
to the festival, hearing that Jesus was on the way to
13 Jerusalem, took palm branches and went out to meet him,
shouting, 'Hosanna! Blessings on him who comes in
the name of the Lord! God bless the king of Israel!'
14 Jesus found a donkey and mounted it, in accordance with
15 the text of Scripture: 'Fear no more, daughter of Zion;
see, your king is coming, mounted on an ass's colt.'
16   At the time his disciples did not understand this, but
after Jesus had been glorified they remembered that this
had been written about him, and that this had happened
17 to him. The people who were present when he called
Lazarus out of the tomb and raised him from the dead
18 told what they had seen and heard. That is why the crowd
went to meet him; they had heard of this sign that he had
19 performed. The Pharisees said to one another, 'You see
you are doing no good at all; why, all the world has gone
after him.'

∗ All four Gospels have this story; but there is no good
evidence that John took it from his predecessors and much
evidence that he did not. Among the peculiarities of his
account notice: (1) his dating of the incident; (2) his mention
of palm branches; (3) the spontaneous action of the pilgrim
crowd; and (4) the disciples' failure to understand.

According to Mark 11: 8 f., it was the crowd accompanying
Jesus into the city who raised the Messianic acclamation. In
John it was the body of pilgrims already in the city who went
out to meet him. And it was this welcome which moved
Jesus to do what he did. For the crowd's greeting was un-
mistakably Messianic. 'Hosanna!' they shouted, doubtless

waving their palm branches, 'God bless the king of Israel [i.e. Messiah]!'. The palm branch was 'a regal symbol', and carrying palms was a recognized mark of homage to a conqueror or a king. The pilgrim crowd were in fact now doing what the crowd in Galilee had tried to do—acclaiming Jesus as a King Messiah after their own hearts. Jesus' response was not a word but a symbolic deed. He *found* an ass (Mark 11: 1–7 tell us how), not a war-horse but the beast of peace. He was proclaiming himself a spiritual Messiah, not a military one; in fact, acting out the great prophecy of Zech. 9: 9 f., 'behold, thy king cometh unto thee...lowly, and riding upon an ass...and he shall speak peace unto the nations'.

But the disciples, missing Jesus' meaning, joined in the crowd's welcome, and those who had witnessed the miracle at Bethany did not keep silent. Small wonder the Pharisees grew alarmed: *why, all the world has gone after him.* (They spoke more truly than they knew!) It was high time they took Caiaphas's advice (11: 49). The time for half measures was past.

12. *The next day*, i.e. after the anointing (which was on Saturday): Palm Sunday, we would say.

13. *palm branches* were used to hail the victorious Simon Maccabee (1 Macc. 13: 51).

Hosanna! (lit. 'save now') is Hebrew for 'Hail'. The words of the first sentence of the Messianic shout come from Ps. 118: 26.

14. *the text of Scripture.* A free version of Zech. 9: 9.

16. *At the time his disciples did not understand.* Cf. 2: 22. Only later, when the Holy Spirit 'lit up' their minds, did the disciples realize that Jesus had fulfilled the prophecy.

19. *all the world.* On the Pharisees' lips, it would mean 'the common rabble'; but for John doubtless it is a prophecy of the coming of all nations to Christ. *

THE REQUEST OF THE GREEKS

20 Among those who went up to worship at the festival were
21 some Greeks. They came to Philip, who was from Bethsaida in Galilee, and said to him, 'Sir, we should like to
22 see Jesus.' So Philip went and told Andrew, and the two
23 of them went to tell Jesus. Then Jesus replied: 'The
24 hour has come for the Son of Man to be glorified. In
truth, in very truth I tell you, a grain of wheat remains a
solitary grain unless it falls into the ground and dies; but
25 if it dies, it bears a rich harvest. The man who loves himself is lost, but he who hates himself in this world will be
26 kept safe for eternal life. If anyone serves me, he must
follow me; where I am, my servant will be. Whoever
serves me will be honoured by my Father.

27 'Now my soul is in turmoil, and what am I to say?
Father, save me from this hour. No, it was for this that I
28 came to this hour. Father, glorify thy name.' A voice
sounded from heaven: 'I have glorified it, and I will glorify
29 it again.' The crowd standing by said it was thunder,
30 while others said, 'An angel has spoken to him.' Jesus re-
31 plied, 'This voice spoke for your sake, not mine. Now is
the hour of judgement for this world; now shall the Prince
32 of this world be driven out. And I shall draw all men to
33 myself, when I am lifted up from the earth.' This he said
to indicate the kind of death he was to die.

34 The people answered, 'Our Law teaches us that the
Messiah continues for ever. What do you mean by saying
that the Son of Man must be lifted up? What Son of Man
35 is this?' Jesus answered them: 'The light is among you
still, but not for long. Go on your way while you have

the light, so that darkness may not overtake you. He who journeys in the dark does not know where he is going. While you have the light, trust to the light, that you may become men of light.' After these words Jesus went away from them into hiding.   36

✻ As the Messiah entered his capital to inaugurate a 'dominion' that should be 'from sea to sea' (Zech. 9: 10), some of 'the scattered children of God' expressed a wish to see him. Gentiles of Greek birth, they had been attracted by the religion of Israel, had become 'Godfearers', and were in the habit of attending the great Jewish festivals. Now they chose as their 'go-between' Philip, a disciple with a Greek name and a Gentile background. When Philip, taking with him his fellow-townsman, Andrew, conveyed the Greeks' request to Jesus, he made the surprising reply, *The hour has come for the Son of Man to be glorified*. But how? Outwardly, by the homage of the Gentiles, of which these are the firstfruits. But also in the deeper sense that the cross, which is the step to the throne of glory, is at hand.

Jesus then uttered the little parable of the corn of wheat (verse 24). 'The way of redemption,' he said in effect, 'is the story of a grain of wheat. Death is the necessary condition of fuller life, of a richer harvest.' Next, he made it clear that this law of life through death applied not only to himself but to his followers. *The man who loves himself is lost, but he who hates himself in this world will be kept safe for eternal life* (verse 25). This saying, richly paralleled in the earlier Gospels, starkly expresses not only the tragedy of self-love but the glory of self-sacrifice—and its reward. Then he added: *If anyone serves me, he must follow me; where I am, my servant will be*. It has been said that *follow me* is the whole of a Christian's duty, as to *be* where Christ is is the whole of his reward.

Then Jesus turns to survey the way of the cross which stretches out before him. (John will not tell the story of his agony in Gethsemane. But, obviously, he knows it, and this is his equivalent.) *Now my soul is in turmoil, and what am I to say? Father, save me from this hour.* But the thought that he may avoid the cross is no sooner uttered than he crushes it out in a word of complete surrender: *No, it was for this that I came to this hour. Father, glorify thy name.* The last four words may be paraphrased: 'Father, complete the revelation of thy holy love, even at the cost of my agony.' It is John's equivalent of 'not what I will, but what thou wilt' (Mark 14: 36).

As Jesus was speaking, there came a sudden clap of thunder, as though in answer. Thunder is represented in the Old Testament as the voice of God; and the same sound could be interpreted as thunder or as the voice of an angel (verse 29). To Jesus, however, it was the divine assurance that, as God had manifested his glorious power in the raising of Lazarus (11: 4), so he would do it again in the death and raising of his Son. It was not for Christ's sake that the heavenly voice had come —he needed no such reassurance—but for the sake of the crowd standing by. (We may compare the Transfiguration where the heavenly voice came not for Jesus' own encouragement, but for the disciples': 'This is my Son, my Beloved; listen to him.' Mark 9: 7.)

But now Jesus began to see in vision his impending grapple with the power of evil and his triumph over him in that death which would draw men, like a magnet, to himself. *Now is the hour of judgement for this world; now shall the Prince of this world be driven out* (verse 31). How is the cross the hour of this world's judgement? Because in it and by it the world's present thraldom to the devil will be shattered and defeated by the victorious obedience of the Son of God. And that death will 'universalize' his mission: *I shall draw all men to myself, when I am lifted up from the earth* (verse 32). Again this favourite word of John's, *lifted up*. It refers primarily here to the cross, as John's note in verse 33 indicates. But it includes also the idea of Christ's exaltation when, as the reigning Lord, he will attract the homage of all men (Phil. 2: 10).

This veiled doctrine of the cross, however, mystifies the

crowd (verses 34 ff.). When Jesus calls himself *the Son of Man*, they rightly suppose him to mean the Messiah. But (they say) *our Law* (i.e. the Scripture) has nothing to say about the removal of the Messiah; on the contrary, it promises that he will abide for ever. *What Son of Man is this?* they ask, perplexedly. Instead of answering their question, Jesus challenges them with a last parable, that of the traveller at sunset (35 f.). 'The light is among you,' he says in effect, 'but only for a brief time. Now or never avail yourselves of it.' His public ministry among his own people is ended. *After these words Jesus went away from them into hiding.* We are ready now for the revelation to his own in the upper room, before he is lifted up on the cross.

23. *The hour*, mentioned as far back as 2: 4, is the hour of his Passion which is also the step to his throne.

24. Paul uses the same illustration in 1 Cor. 15: 36 f.

25. There are Synoptic parallels to this saying. The glory of self-sacrifice enunciated in it finds little or no place in Greek thought. Here Gospel ethics leave Greek ones far behind.

26. The glory of service is also a theme which bulks large in the earlier Gospels.

27. John also shows his knowledge of the agony at 18: 1, 11. Here *Now my soul is in turmoil* corresponds to 'My heart is ready to break with grief' (Mark 14: 34), and *save me from this hour* to Mark 14: 35.

28. *A voice sounded from heaven.* Thrice in the ministry—at the Baptism, at the Transfiguration and here, just before the cross—we hear of a heavenly voice. The bystanders did not understand the voices. We should say that their messages were subjective since they had a meaning only for him to whom they were addressed; but objective also, because they were true voices of God.

31. *the Prince of this world*: the devil. Cf. 2 Cor. 4: 4 and Eph. 2: 2. Paul also saw the cross as Christ's victorious deathgrapple with the powers of evil (Col. 2: 15, and compare Luke 10: 18).

32. Jesus' death and its manner will universalize his work. History has proved him right. The cross of Christ has been a magnet, 'more than all his miracles'.

34. *the Messiah continues for ever.* See Isa. 9: 7 and Ezek. 37: 25.

35 f. In interpreting the parable of the traveller at sunset we must remember Christ's claim to be the light of the world. ✳

EPILOGUE TO THE PUBLIC MINISTRY

37 In spite of the many signs which Jesus had performed in
38 their presence they would not believe in him, for the prophet Isaiah's utterance had to be fulfilled: 'Lord, who has believed what we reported, and to whom has the
39 Lord's power been revealed?' So it was that they could
40 not believe, for there is another saying of Isaiah's: 'He has blinded their eyes and dulled their minds, lest they should see with their eyes, and perceive with their minds, and
41 turn to me to heal them.' Isaiah said this because he saw his glory and spoke about him.

42   For all that, even among those in authority a number believed in him, but would not acknowledge him on account of the Pharisees, for fear of being banned from
43 the synagogue. For they valued their reputation with men rather than the honour which comes from God.

44 So Jesus cried aloud: 'When a man believes in me, he
45 believes in him who sent me rather than in me; seeing me,
46 he sees him who sent me. I have come into the world as light, so that no one who has faith in me should remain in
47 darkness. But if anyone hears my words and pays no regard to them, I am not his judge; I have not come to
48 judge the world, but to save the world. There is a judge

for the man who rejects me and does not accept my words; the word that I spoke will be his judge on the last day. I do not speak on my own authority, but the 49 Father who sent me has himself commanded me what to say and how to speak. I know that his commands are 50 eternal life. What the Father has said to me, therefore— that is what I speak.'

✻ In this epilogue to Jesus' public ministry John first quotes scripture to show that Christ's rejection had been prophesied in the Old Testament; and then he makes Jesus briefly summarize his teaching.

In spite of the many signs which Jesus had performed in their presence they would not believe in him. Why? John's reply is that the unbelief of the Jews was no accident but the fulfilment of prophecy. He begins by quoting words from the famous prophecy about the Servant of the Lord despised and rejected by men (Isa. 53: 1. Here *what we reported* refers to Jesus' preaching, as *the Lord's power* to his miracles). Then he adds words from Isaiah's vision of the Lord (Isa. 6: 10), which Jesus himself, according to Mark 4: 12, had used to explain Jewish unbelief: *He has blinded their eyes and dulled their minds.* This second passage serves to stress 'the divine inevitability' of the Jews' unbelief. If the application strikes us as harsh, John is reflecting on the sad fact that God's own people had deliberately rejected his Son the Messiah. Let us also remember that Jewish 'determinism' is not nearly so bad as it sounds. The Jews could say, 'The Lord hardened Pharaoh's heart' when we would say 'Under God's providence Pharaoh hardened his heart', Pharaoh being free to respond to Moses' appeal. Just so, although John tells us (verse 39) that the Jews *could not believe,* three verses later he records that a number of important Jews did believe in him—even if they had not the courage of their convictions because man's honour meant more to them than God's.

In the concluding verses (verses 44–50) John makes Jesus summarize his message. None of it is now new to us. (Belief in Christ is belief in God. To see Christ is to see the Father. Christ is the light of the world. His primary purpose is not judgement but salvation. To reject Jesus is to come under the judgement of God, etc. All this we can parallel in teaching already given, and verses 44, 47 and 48 reflect teaching given in the Synoptic Gospels.)

The point of it all is that faith does not rest in Jesus but in the Father who sent him. Consequently, the rejection of Jesus by the Jews was not simply a fulfilment of prophecy; it was the *denial of God*, for which the Jews must abide the consequences.

41. *Isaiah said this because he saw his glory.* Is it enough to explain this by saying that to John, as to the rest of the New Testament writers, the Old Testament spoke of Christ? In Isa. 52: 13 the prophet predicts of the rejected Servant of the Lord that he will be 'exalted and lifted up', using the same verbs as John does. May we then say that the conception of the cross as the glory goes back to Isaiah?

44. *Jesus cried aloud.* This does not mean that on a particular occasion Jesus spoke the words that follow. It means: 'This is the content of the message of Jesus' (Dodd). ✻

Farewell Discourses

INSTRUCTION OF THE DISCIPLES

✻ Christ's revelation to the world is over. In the next five chapters we have his revelation to the disciples. As chapters 2–12 illustrate, 'The real light was in the world...but the world did not recognize him' (1:9f.); chapters 13–20 illustrate, 'To all who did receive him...he gave the right to become children of God' (1: 12 f.).

Two questions arise here. (1) What is the significance of these chapters in the structure of the Gospel? (2) How far can they be accepted as authentic?

(1) In John's Gospel an act of Christ (a work) is usually followed by teaching (a word) which elucidates its meaning. Thus the miracle of the feeding is followed by the discourse on the bread of life. Chapters 13–20 differ only in this, that now the teaching *precedes* the action (18–20). For, as John sees it, the cross is the supreme 'sign'.

(2) How far are these farewell discourses historical? We may be sure that the events of that night made an indelible impression on those who were in the upper room, as the Beloved Disciple was, and that the earlier Gospels have not preserved the whole story.

Next, there is an appropriate and natural progression in the discourses themselves: first, talk with individual disciples, then Jesus' soliloquy, then the great prayer.

Most important of all, we find in the discourses not only sayings resembling those in the Synoptic Gospels (e.g. 13: 16, 20, 21, 38) but *expansions* of topics—the death and return of Jesus, the disciples' mission, the certainty of persecution, the promised help of the Holy Spirit, etc.—which, according to the earlier Gospels, formed part of Christ's private instruction of the Twelve (see especially Mark 13 and Matt. 10).

On the other hand, the thoughts in the discourses have not only passed through the very individual mind of the evangelist, but reflect his Christian experience. John 14: 26 probably takes us as near the truth as may be: 'The Holy Spirit whom the Father will send in my name, will teach you everything, and will call to mind all that I have told you.' What we have in the discourses is (1) Christ's own words; (2) the memory of the disciples; and (3) the interpretation of the Spirit. If it be true that 'Christ in the apostles interpreted his finished work as truly as in his lifetime he interpreted his unfinished work' (P. T. Forsyth), we should not undervalue the contribution of the Spirit.

After the foot-washing and the departure of Judas, the discourses may be summarized thus:

(*a*) The first instruction (Christ's departure and return): 13: 31 — 14: 31.

(*b*) The second instruction (Christ and his church) 15: 1 — 16: 33.

(*c*) The great prayer: chapter 17. ✳

THE FOOT-WASHING

13 IT WAS BEFORE the Passover festival. Jesus knew that his hour had come and he must leave this world and go to the Father. He had always loved his own who were in the world, and now he was to show the full extent of his love.

2 The devil had already put it into the mind of Judas son 3 of Simon Iscariot to betray him. During supper, Jesus, well aware that the Father had entrusted everything to him, and that he had come from God and was going back 4 to God, rose from table, laid aside his garments, and taking 5 a towel, tied it round him. Then he poured water into a basin, and began to wash his disciples' feet and to wipe them with the towel.

6 When it was Simon Peter's turn, Peter said to him, 7 'You, Lord, washing my feet?' Jesus replied, 'You do not understand now what I am doing, but one day you will.' 8 Peter said, 'I will never let you wash my feet.' 'If I do not wash you,' Jesus replied, 'you are not in fellowship with 9 me.' 'Then, Lord,' said Simon Peter, 'not my feet only; wash my hands and head as well!'

10 Jesus said, 'A man who has bathed needs no further washing; he is altogether clean; and you are clean, though

not every one of you.' He added the words 'not every   11
one of you' because he knew who was going to betray
him.

After washing their feet and taking his garments again,   12
he sat down. 'Do you understand', he asked, 'what I have
done for you? You call me "Master" and "Lord", and   13
rightly so, for that is what I am. Then if I, your Lord and   14
Master, have washed your feet, you also ought to wash
one another's feet. I have set you an example: you are   15
to do as I have done for you. In very truth I tell you, a   16
servant is not greater than his master, nor a messenger
than the one who sent him. If you know this, happy are   17
you if you act upon it.

'I am not speaking about all of you; I know whom I   18
have chosen. But there is a text of Scripture to be fulfilled: "He who eats bread with me has turned against
me." I tell you this now, before the event, that when it   19
happens you may believe that I am what I am. In very   20
truth I tell you, he who receives any messenger of mine
receives me; receiving me, he receives the One who sent
me.'

✻ The earlier evangelists record the institution of the Lord's
Supper. John does not, doubtless because he did not wish
to divulge 'the Christian mystery' to non-Christian ears.
Instead, he recounts an incident, unrecorded in the earlier
Gospels—unless Luke 22: 27 is an echo of it.

First, John sets the scene, chronologically and theologically.
It was just before the Passover when Jesus, knowing that his
hour of death was nigh—Judas having accepted the diabolical
suggestion of his betrayal—held a last meal with his own.
When it was already in progress, Jesus, conscious of his divine
origin and destiny, and aware that God had entrusted him

with the whole work of salvation, gave his disciples a final and complete proof of his love.

Perhaps contention among his disciples (cf. Luke 22: 24 f.) moved him to do what he now did. Suddenly he rose from table, put off his coat, procured a basin and water, and was on his knees washing the disciples' feet and wiping them with a towel. The Son of God had literally taken the form of a servant (Phil. 2: 7). John does not tell us with which of the disciples he began. We only know that when it came to his turn, Peter said, 'You, Lord, washing my feet?', no doubt drawing up his feet in horror. 'Yes, Peter, and you will know the reason why one day.' 'Never!' 'Then if I do not wash you, you are not in fellowship with me.' Peter, half comprehending, cried, 'Wash me all over'. He asked too much, not knowing that he was already fully cleansed, as Jesus now told him, 'A man who has bathed needs no further cleansing'. But he added that no amount of washing would cleanse one of their number who had become the devil's agent.

When Jesus had 'taken' his garments again and the acted parable was over, he bade them do what he himself had done, following his example. Servants were not greater than their master; yet as his envoys they would represent him. And uttering the 'benediction of ministry' (verse 17), he turned to talk of his betrayer.

Was the whole episode, as some hold, simply an acted parable whose theme was the glory of service? This is part of the truth, but far from the whole of it—or else in that mysterious dialogue with Peter Jesus is simply obscuring the parable's plain lesson.

Let us look at it again. Recall first that all is enacted, so to say, in the shadow of the cross and that the washer of the disciples' feet is the one destined to take away the world's sins. Consider next the verbs which John uses to describe Jesus' actions. Jesus 'lays aside' his garments and, the washing over, 'takes them again'. These are the very verbs which the Good Shepherd had used of his death and resurrection (10: 11, 15,

17 f.). Above all, remember that the motif of the whole story is cleansing and that Jesus said to Peter, 'If I do not wash you, you are not in fellowship with me'. The deeper meaning then is that there is no place in his fellowship for those who have not been cleansed by his atoning death. The episode dramatically symbolizes the truth enunciated in 1 John 1: 7, 'We are being cleansed from every sin by the blood of Jesus'.

Many people today would like to be Christians but see no need of the cross. They are ready to admire Jesus' life and to praise the sublimity of his moral teaching, but they cannot bring themselves to believe that Christ died for their sins, and that without that death they would be lost in sin. This, as Brunner has said, is one of the prime 'scandals' of Christianity for modern man—and the very heart of the apostolic Gospel.

The subsequent summons to humble service (verses 13 f.) is then the corollary of what Christ has done for his disciples. Because they have been redeemed by the death of the Servant Son of God, they must show their gratitude in the service of others. When Jesus bids them wash one another's feet, it is the spirit—the moral essence—of his act, and not the letter of it, that matters. Not crowns and coronets, but towels and basins are the insignia of the Saviour's kingdom, and he best honours the Son of God who is prepared to stoop and serve.

1. *before the Passover*. The Last Supper may well have been a Passover meal, but (according to John) it was not a regular one, since it was held before the official date.

2. *The devil*. Cf. Luke 22: 3.

7. *one day you will*. After the coming of the Spirit.

10. Some MSS, as the N.E.B. footnote says, read 'needs only to wash his feet'. If we accept this longer reading, the meaning will be as follows. Guests usually bathed before going to a feast; but on arrival washed the travel-stains from their feet. So the disciples, already cleansed by their fellowship with Christ, need only to have their slighter faults removed.

16. Cf. Matt. 10: 40, Luke 6: 40.

18. Ps. 41: 9, *has turned against me* is literally, 'has lifted up his heel against me'. The picture is of a horse kicking its owner while it is being fed.

19. *I am what I am.* See note on 8: 24.

20. Yet another saying found in the earlier Gospels. See Luke 10: 16; Mark 9: 37; Matt. 10: 40.

In the previous verse Jesus has made the divine claim *I am what I am*, implying his union with the Father. Here he emphasizes his union with his messengers. Those therefore who welcome them are welcoming both him and his Father. In the Christian mission it is God himself whom men encounter. ✻

THE DEPARTURE OF JUDAS

21 After saying this, Jesus exclaimed in deep agitation of spirit, 'In truth, in very truth I tell you, one of you is
22 going to betray me.' The disciples looked at one another in bewilderment: whom could he be speaking of?
23 One of them, the disciple he loved, was reclining close
24 beside Jesus. So Simon Peter nodded to him and said,
25 'Ask who it is he means.' That disciple, as he reclined, leaned back close to Jesus and asked, 'Lord, who is it?'
26 Jesus replied, 'It is the man to whom I give this piece of bread when I have dipped it in the dish.' Then, after dipping it in the dish, he took it out and gave it to Judas
27 son of Simon Iscariot. As soon as Judas had received it Satan entered him. Jesus said to him, 'Do quickly what
28 you have to do.' No one at the table understood what he
29 meant by this. Some supposed that, as Judas was in charge of the common purse, Jesus was telling him to buy what was needed for the festival, or to make some gift to
30 the poor. Judas, then, received the bread and went out. It was night.

✳ While Judas was still in the upper room, Jesus remained ill at ease. With his announcement that his betrayer was one of their number, all began to look incredulously at each other.

To understand what followed, remember that all would be reclining sideways at table, propped up on their left elbows, with Jesus the host at the centre. So when Peter appealed to the Beloved Disciple (here mentioned for the first time) for a hint of the betrayer, we must picture him on Christ's right, with his head slightly below his master's, and therefore perfectly placed to receive a confidential disclosure. Jesus told him that a coming gesture would disclose the man's identity. It is implied that none but the Beloved Disciple heard Christ's word.

In the East it is a mark of special favour for the host to dip a piece of bread in the common sauce-dish and hand it to a guest, as Jesus now did to Judas. If this giving of the sop was a last appeal to Judas, with its rejection Judas deliberately became the devil's agent. His unmasking by Jesus crystallized his decision to do the devil's work. Something of the tension in Jesus' soul appears in his command to Judas: *Do quickly what you have to do* (cf. Luke 12: 49).

The rest of the disciples, says the evangelist, missing the meaning of this by-play, supposed their Master was instructing Judas, as purse-bearer, about some purchase or a gift for the poor (a Passover custom). *Judas* at once *went out. It was night.* (Are there three more dramatic words in literature?) As the door closed behind him, all caught a glimpse of the enveloping night—fit symbol for his dark business. He was going out from the light of the world into 'outer darkness'.

22. In Mark 14: 18, 20 we find a general prediction that one of the Twelve will betray Jesus. In Matt. 26: 25 Jesus expressly names Judas. According to John, only the Beloved Disciple was let into the secret of his identity.

23. *the disciple he loved.* In our view, John son of Zebedee— see pages 12 f. ✳

GLORIFICATION AND DENIAL

31 When he had gone out Jesus said, 'Now the Son of Man
32 is glorified, and in him God is glorified. If God is glorified in him, God will also glorify him in himself; and he
33 will glorify him now. My children, for a little longer I
am with you; then you will look for me, and, as I told
the Jews, I tell you now, where I am going you cannot
34 come. I give you a new commandment: love one another;
35 as I have loved you, so you are to love one another. If
there is this love among you, then all will know that you
are my disciples.'

36   Simon Peter said to him, 'Lord, where are you going?'
Jesus replied, 'Where I am going you cannot follow me
37 now, but one day you will.' Peter said, 'Lord, why
cannot I follow you now? I will lay down my life for
38 you.' Jesus answered, 'Will you indeed lay down your
life for me? I tell you in very truth, before the cock crows
you will have denied me three times.

* With Judas gone, Jesus' spirits rose and with a note of
triumph he cried *Now the Son of Man is glorified*, as though
his Passion were already past and his glory disclosed in it. He
added, *and in him God is glorified*. How? Because Jesus by his
obedience unto death has revealed the true nature of God.
With the next verse (31) however the tense changes to a
future: *God will...glorify him* (Jesus) *in himself*. The glory of
the cross will be crowned by the Father taking up Jesus into
his own glory and Godhead. When? *Now*. He is thinking of
his victory over death and the advent of the Spirit (who will
'glorify' him, 16: 14), to follow on his Passion.

But Jesus' way to glory involves separation from his disciples who must stay on in the world. So to them, as the nucleus of the New Israel, he delivers the new *Law*: *I give you a new commandment: love one another; as I have loved you, so you are to love one another.* But did not the old *Torah* (Lev. 19: 18) bid them love their neighbour? How is the *commandment new*? Because there is to be a new love-circle depending on a new love-centre, Christ. And was not the love of Christ's friends for Christ's sake a new thing in the world? What is to be the pattern and inspiration of this new love? It is: *as I have loved you.* The allusion is to the foot-washing and so to Christ's death which it symbolized. Their love is to show the same self-giving quality as Jesus had shown in going to the cross for them. Such love, he says, will be the distinguishing badge of his followers in the world.

It was a spiritual journey—a journey to the Father via the cross—of which Jesus had spoken. Hence Peter's puzzled question (verse 36), *Lord, where are you going?* When Jesus, hinting at Peter's future martyrdom, replies, 'You will follow me one day, but not now.' Peter asks, 'Why not now? I am ready to lay down my life for you.' He is undertaking to do for Jesus what the Good Shepherd does for his sheep (10: 11). Poor, loyal, ignorant, impetuous Peter! He has to learn not only what a fall awaits him before the dawn breaks, but also that, until his Master has trodden the way alone, he cannot become 'the true and living Way' for all his followers, Peter included.

32. The words *If God is glorified in him* do not occur in many of our early good MSS and should probably be omitted.

33. *My children.* A tender form of address which John often uses in his First Letter.

as I told the Jews. See 7: 33 and 8: 21.

38. For Jesus' prediction of Peter's denial see also Mark 14: 30 and Luke 22: 34.

before the cock crows. See the note on 18: 27. ✷

THE TRUE AND LIVING WAY

14 'Set your troubled hearts at rest. Trust in God always;
2 trust also in me. There are many dwelling-places in my
Father's house; if it were not so I should have told you;
for I am going there on purpose to prepare a place for
3 you. And if I go and prepare a place for you, I shall come
again and receive you to myself, so that where I am you
4, 5 may be also; and my way there is known to you.' Thomas
said, 'Lord, we do not know where you are going, so
6 how can we know the way?' Jesus replied, 'I am the
way; I am the truth and I am life; no one comes to the
Father except by me.

7 'If you knew me you would know my Father too.
From now on you do know him; you have seen him.'
8 Philip said to him, 'Lord, show us the Father and we ask
9 no more.' Jesus answered, 'Have I been all this time with
you, Philip, and you still do not know me? Anyone who
has seen me has seen the Father. Then how can you say,
10 "Show us the Father"? Do you not believe that I am in
the Father, and the Father in me? I am not myself the
source of the words I speak to you: it is the Father who
11 dwells in me doing his own work. Believe me when I
say that I am in the Father and the Father in me; or else
12 accept the evidence of the deeds themselves. In truth,
in very truth I tell you, he who has faith in me will do
what I am doing; and he will do greater things still
13 because I am going to the Father. Indeed anything you
ask in my name I will do, so that the Father may be
14 glorified in the Son. If you ask anything in my name I
will do it.

✻ Chapter 14 forms the bulk of what we have called 'the First Instruction'. Its main themes are: the departure and return of Jesus; his revelation of the Father; the union of the Son, and of believers in him, with the Father; the power of prayer; the promise of the 'Paraclete'; and the obedience of believers to Christ in love.

Despite his coming departure, Jesus bids his disciples not to despond. *Set your troubled hearts at rest*, he says. The secret of the untroubled heart is firmer faith—faith not only in God but in himself. In his *Father's house* there is room for all, and he is going ahead to prepare for them. We may recall how Jesus, the day before—see Mark 14: 12–16—had sent two of his disciples ahead to secure 'a large room upstairs' for the Last Supper. They did not 'know the way', but had to follow the owner. Arriving, they found everything 'prepared', as Jesus had said. It looks as if here Jesus has made the disciples' journey of the previous day into a parable of eternity, in which the upper room foreshadows the home of God with its many habitations.

But the Lord promises also to return himself—*I shall come again and receive you to myself*. Are we to think of his coming to the disciple at death or at some second coming? Since none of the other four sayings about Christ's coming (14: 18, 28; 16: 16 and 16: 22) refers to the second advent, the odds seem against that meaning here. If the reference is to the believer's death, we may recall that Paul hoped to pass at death into the presence of his Lord (Phil. 1: 23; 2 Cor. 5: 8).

When Christ declares that his *way* (to the Father) is known to them, Thomas demurs (he is evidently thinking of a journey from land to land), only to receive the majestic rejoinder *I am the way; I am the truth and I am life*. The literal rendering is, 'I am the way, the truth and the life'. We may take this to mean: Jesus is *the way* to God because he is *the truth*, i.e. the personal self-revelation of God, and because he is *the life*, i.e. the vital energy which sustains men on their way to him. But very attractive is the suggestion, made long ago and accepted by Moffatt, that the nouns *truth* and *life* define the *way*—in other words, are used adjectivally, so that the meaning is, 'I am the true and living way' (cf. Jer. 29: 11 where 'a latter end and a hope' means 'a hoped-for latter end'). Jesus is the way that leads to the only real knowledge of God and so alone leads to life. For *no one comes to the Father except by me.* This does not condemn all seekers after God; but it does assert that Jesus is alone the way to the Father. (And is there not all the difference between merely accepting God's existence and believing in him as a heavenly Father?)

In the next verse (7) we prefer the reading in the N.E.B.'s footnote: *If you know me you will know my Father too.* Instead of a reproach we get a promise, and so are prepared for the immediate resolution of the future into a present: *From now on you do know him; you have seen him.*

At this point Philip asks for such a revelation of God as Moses had enjoyed (Exod. 24: 9–11; 33: 18): *Lord, show us the Father and we ask no more.* He would like Jesus to pull aside the veil separating the seen from the unseen—to disclose a great Father-figure! But such a theophany is quite unnecessary. 'Have you been all this time in my company,' Jesus asks, 'and yet you have not yet realized that I am the image of the unseen Father?' The complete revelation of God is present for Philip's eyes to see, his hands to handle. Has he been so blind as not to glimpse the secret of his Master's being—a Father in whom he lives, who lives in him? *I am not myself the source of the words I speak to you: it is the Father who dwells in me doing his own work.* But, he adds, if this makes too great a demand on your credence, then *accept the evidence of the deeds themselves.* 'Miracle-faith' may not be the highest sort; but better believe because of miracles than not at all.

Then, looking into the future, Jesus promises that the believer in himself will do even *greater things* than he himself is doing. *Greater*, quantitatively. Jesus' works were inevitably confined to Palestine and the Jews. Theirs will be the harvest of the Gentiles. These works, however, will only be possible because of Jesus' own work—because he goes to the Father by way of the cross.

This, then, is his promise to them, and in so far as the disciples *pray in his name*, i.e. in accordance with his character and will, Jesus, from his place of power with the Father, will answer their petitions, so that *the Father may be glorified in the Son*.

1. The A.V. translation 'You believe in God', 'Believe also in me' is also possible.

2. *dwelling-places*. The Greek word might mean 'stopping-places', and so convey a picture of inns along a road where travellers may rest. But in verse 23 the same word clearly means a permanent dwelling, not a temporary halt. The idea is therefore of a hospitable house with many rooms rather than of a journey with many stages. ✳

THE OTHER ADVOCATE

'If you love me you will obey my commands; and I will 15,16 ask the Father, and he will give you another to be your Advocate, who will be with you for ever—the Spirit of 17 truth. The world cannot receive him, because the world neither sees nor knows him; but you know him, because he dwells with you and is in you. I will not leave you 18 bereft; I am coming back to you. In a little while the 19 world will see me no longer, but you will see me; because I live, you too will live; then you will know that I 20 am in my Father, and you in me and I in you. The man 21 who has received my commands and obeys them—he it is who loves me; and he who loves me will be loved by my Father; and I will love him and disclose myself to him.'

Judas asked him—the other Judas, not Iscariot—'Lord, 22 what can have happened, that you mean to disclose yourself to us alone and not to the world?' Jesus replied, 'Any- 23

one who loves me will heed what I say; then my Father will love him, and we will come to him and make our
24 dwelling with him; but he who does not love me does not heed what I say. And the word you hear is not mine:
25 it is the word of the Father who sent me. I have told you
26 all this while I am still here with you; but your Advocate, the Holy Spirit whom the Father will send in my name, will teach you everything, and will call to mind all that I have told you.

27 'Peace is my parting gift to you, my own peace, such as the world cannot give. Set your troubled hearts at
28 rest, and banish your fears. You heard me say, "I am going away, and coming back to you." If you loved me you would have been glad to hear that I was going to the
29 Father; for the Father is greater than I. I have told you now, beforehand, so that when it happens you may have faith.

30 'I shall not talk much longer with you, for the Prince
31 of this world approaches. He has no rights over me; but the world must be shown that I love the Father, and do exactly as he commands; so up, let us go forward!

* Let the disciples show their love for him by obedience, and he will ask the Father to give them *another to be* their *Advocate*, or helper. This is the *Spirit of truth*, the Spirit who gives knowledge of divine reality. His ministry (unlike Christ's) will be permanent, though the unspiritual world will be quite unresponsive to it. How different it will be with the disciples, because the Spirit will abide in their fellowship and be in them (verses 15-17).

His going does not mean that they are to be 'orphans', for he is *coming back*—in the Resurrection. If the world has seen the last of him, the disciples will see him in his risen power—

which is the pledge of their own eternal life. Then they will recognize him as truly the mediator between God and men and share, through him, in his life with the Father. But obedience (verse 21) is the true test of devotion; and it will be rewarded with the Father's love and the love and self-revelation of Jesus himself.

These promises, however, disappoint *the other Judas* (verse 22). He thinks it would be much more impressive if Jesus were to manifest himself so that the whole *world*, and not simply the disciples, could see him. Disregarding this demand and repeating his own for obedience, Jesus assures them that both the Father and the Son will make their *dwelling* with the obedient disciple (verse 23). This is not a reference to the Second Advent or to the Resurrection but to the permanent abiding of the Godhead with the believer—the spiritual experience which John describes in 1 John 1: 3.

Let this assurance suffice now. The Holy Spirit whom the Father will send to take Christ's place will complete the unfinished teaching and remind them of all the truths he has taught them.

Then (verse 27), like a man making his will before death, Jesus bequeaths to them his own *peace*, that perfect inward serenity which comes from reconciliation with God: no conventional Hebrew *shalōm* or farewell but a true spiritual gift. Let them banish all their fears. They have his promise—it is *au revoir*, not farewell; for if he must go, he will come back. To true love this would have been cause for joy (he says), for his destination is the source of supreme power, the Father himself. He is telling them all this in advance so that the event may confirm their faith. But now time presses: near at hand is the power who *de facto* (if not *de jure*) rules the world and who must be confronted. Not that he has any hold over Jesus. But events must take their sombre course so that the world may learn the love and obedience of Jesus.

16. *Advocate*. The Greek word *paraklētos* means literally 'one called to one's side', a helper, and since the context of its

use is often the law-court, an advocate. The farewell discourses refer five times to this 'Paraclete'. He is primarily the Spirit who works in the redemption Christ brings, confirming and instructing the Church, and pricking the conscience of the world. He comes as Christ's other self, not so much to supply his absence as to confirm his presence.

17. *he dwells with you and is in you.* The present tenses have a future sense. During the Incarnation the Spirit was *with* men in Christ; since then Christ has been *in* men by the Spirit.

19. *because I live, you too will live.* Neither John nor the New Testament generally teaches man's natural immortality. Eternal life is the gift of God in Christ; and our hope of it is bound up with the living Christ. Because he lives, we who are bound to him by faith, will live also.

21. *I will...disclose myself to him*: as a spiritual presence.

22. *the other Judas.* Judas the son of James (Luke 6: 18, Acts 1: 13).

26. This second saying about the teaching role of the Paraclete in the Church finds admirable illustration in John's Gospel itself which is 'a living and Christian exegesis (exposition) of the words of Jesus preserved in the early tradition of the Church, an exegesis which the writer claims to be inspired by the possession of the Holy Spirit' (Hoskyns).

28. *the Father is greater than I.* Cf. 10: 30. The Son is less than the Father as one sent is less than the sender.

30. *The Prince of this world*: the devil.

31. *so up, let us go forward.* Cf. Mark 14: 42. The words seem to imply that at this point Jesus and his disciples left the upper room and that what follows was spoken on the way to Gethsemane. Those who cannot believe this rearrange—inserting 15 and 16 before 14: 31*a*. C. H. Dodd suggests that at 14: 31 the journey really began—in spirit, if not in actual fact. With these words Jesus deliberately braced himself to confront the devil. As an act of will this was a real, if a spiritual, departure, and fitly concludes a dialogue which has been concerned with his departure. ✳

SECOND INSTRUCTION (CHRIST AND HIS CHURCH):
15: 1 — 16: 33

✻ The second instruction handles more fully themes treated
in the first, especially the relation of the disciples to Christ
after his return to them, and the work of the Holy Spirit.
More definitely than the first it looks into the future, since it
deals with the internal life of the Church, the treatment
Christians may expect from the world, and the Church's
dependence on the historic revelation, as interpreted by the
Spirit of truth. ✻

THE TRUE VINE

'I am the real vine, and my Father is the gardener. Every **15** 1, 2
barren branch of mine he cuts away; and every fruiting
branch he cleans, to make it more fruitful still. You have 3
already been cleansed by the word that I spoke to you.
Dwell in me, as I in you. No branch can bear fruit by 4
itself, but only if it remains united with the vine; no more
can you bear fruit, unless you remain united with me.

'I am the vine, and you the branches. He who dwells 5
in me, as I dwell in him, bears much fruit; for apart from
me you can do nothing. He who does not dwell in me 6
is thrown away like a withered branch. The withered
branches are heaped together, thrown on the fire, and
burnt.

'If you dwell in me, and my words dwell in you, ask 7
what you will, and you shall have it. This is my Father's 8
glory, that you may bear fruit in plenty and so be my
disciples. As the Father has loved me, so I have loved you. 9
Dwell in my love. If you heed my commands, you will 10
dwell in my love, as I have heeded my Father's commands
and dwell in his love.

11 'I have spoken thus to you, so that my joy may be in
12 you, and your joy complete. This is my commandment:
13 love one another, as I have loved you. There is no greater
    love than this, that a man should lay down his life for his
14 friends. You are my friends, if you do what I command
15 you. I call you servants no longer; a servant does not
    know what his master is about. I have called you friends,
    because I have disclosed to you everything that I heard
16 from my Father. You did not choose me: I chose you. I
    appointed you to go on and bear fruit, fruit that shall last;
    so that the Father may give you all that you ask in my name.
17 This is my commandment to you: love one another.

✵ What inspired this allegorical parable of the vine and its
branches? Was it the sight of the great golden vine carved
over the Temple gate which caught Jesus' eye as the little
band made its way to Gethsemane? Or was it wine on the
table at the Last Supper? Whichever it was, to understand its
opening claim we must recall those Old Testament passages
where Israel is pictured as the vine of God (especially Ps. 80,
where God's people is compared to a vine God brought out
of Egypt and is even called 'the son of man'). But Israel, for
all God's tending, had not been the vine he meant it to be. It
had become degenerate, and now Jesus the Son of Man proclaims that the purpose of God entrusted to Israel is being
fulfilled in himself. He embodies the true Israel, the new and
true People of God.

Then, using the language of vine-growers, he describes that
living union between himself and his disciples on which rests
the future of the new fellowship he is founding. He speaks of
pruning, cleaning and fruit-bearing; there is talk of barren
branches (we think of Judas, type of the faithless disciple) and
branches needing to be cleaned before they bear fruit (we
think of Peter). But the pith and point of the parable comes

at verse 4: *Dwell in me, as I in you. No branch can bear fruit by itself, but only if it remains united with the vine; no more can you bear fruit, unless you remain united with me.* (Just so Paul speaks of the body and its members in 1 Cor. 12 and Rom. 12, in order to teach a similar truth.) Initially cleansed by his *word*—the divine revelation he has given them—the disciples' salvation depends on their maintaining that living union with their Lord. Here we reach the heart not of the parable alone but of Christianity itself. *Dwell in me, as I in you.* From this springs all depth of devotion, all effective Christian service.

It is to be noted (verse 5) that Christ is the *whole* vine (not merely the stem, as we might suppose). The disciples, as branches, are part of him, and, to be effective, must completely depend on him. Failure to do this means *withered branches*, fated to be thrown on the fire and burnt. Such disciples, by severing themselves from the source of life, have condemned themselves. On the other hand, to *dwell in* Christ is to have the secret of effective prayer: *If you dwell in me, and my words dwell in you, ask what you will, and you shall have it.* A staggering promise, till you look at the if-clause. If his disciples truly dwell in him, letting his teaching guide their lives, their prayers cannot fail because they can ask nothing contrary to God's will. *This is my Father's glory, that you may bear fruit in plenty and so be my disciples.* What is meant by fruit-bearing? Effective discipleship, effective alike in prayer and preaching, in work and service. Such fruitfulness redounds to the Father's glory. Cf. Matt. 5: 16.

Here (verse 9) the vine-growing images shade away into the plainer language of love. The measure of the Father's love for the Son is the measure of Christ's love for the disciples. Let them stay on in the shelter of his love for them; and the secret of such continuance is obedience to Christ's commands —those commands which can be summed up in the sovereign one of *agapē*—a self-giving love like Christ's own (cf. 13: 34). He reminds them (verse 13) that the love, to which he calls them, is to be measured by his own giving of his life for them.

There is no greater love than this, that a man should lay down his life for his friends. Sacrifice of life for one's friends is here commended as the highest love. Some people have therefore contrasted this saying unfavourably with Rom. 5: 8 where Paul says: 'Christ died for us while we were yet sinners, and that is God's own proof of his love towards us.' But this criticism is hardly fair; for (1) Jesus happens for the moment to be speaking to his *friends* of the supreme pledge of his love he is about to give them; and (2) elsewhere (6: 51) he says that his sacrifice is 'for the life of the world'.

The word *friends* moves Jesus to draw out the difference between slaves and friends. (At 13: 16 he had called them slaves or servants. Now he promotes them.) A slave obeys his master without being allowed to know the reason for his lord's action. But a friend is let into his master's secrets, as Christ's disciples have been let into his, which are his heavenly Father's. (We think of Gen. 18: 17 where the Lord says to Abraham, 'the friend of God', 'Shall I hide from Abraham that which I do?')

Nothing in all this, comments Jesus (verse 16), is the result of the disciples' own initiative. *You did not choose me: I chose you.* All initiative is Christ's; our action is all response. But, as he now says, all such election, or choice, is for *service*: *I appointed you to go on and bear fruit, fruit that shall last.* The *fruit* which Jesus has in mind here must be the fruit of success in their apostolic labours. The end and purpose of it all is *that the Father may give you all that you ask in my name*; that is, that the Father may grant all prayers of theirs made in accordance with Christ's character and will. And once again Christ reiterates the commandment of love.

2. *barren branch.* Judas was in the vine, 'in Christ', a branch not bearing fruit; and the Father had taken him away (Temple).

7. *words.* The sayings of Jesus which make up *the word* (or revelation) of verse 3.

11. *my joy.* The joy of unbroken communion with the Father. ✳

THE HATRED OF THE WORLD

'If the world hates you, it hated me first, as you know 18
well. If you belonged to the world, the world would 19
love its own; but because you do not belong to the world,
because I have chosen you out of the world, for that reason
the world hates you. Remember what I said: "A servant 20
is not greater than his master." As they persecuted me,
they will persecute you; they will follow your teaching
as little as they have followed mine. It is on my account 21
that they will treat you thus, because they do not know
the One who sent me.

'If I had not come and spoken to them, they would not 22
be guilty of sin; but now they have no excuse for their
sin: he who hates me, hates my Father. If I had not 23,24
worked among them and accomplished what no other
man has done, they would not be guilty of sin; but now
they have both seen and hated both me and my Father.
However, this text in their Law had to come true: "They 25
hated me without reason."

'But when your Advocate has come, whom I will send 26
you from the Father—the Spirit of truth that issues from
the Father—he will bear witness to me. And you also are 27
my witnesses, because you have been with me from the
first.

* Jesus now turns to warn his little band how they will fare
in the world. The *world* (a word occurring six times in the
first two verses) bears its characteristically Johannine meaning
—'human society as it organizes itself apart from God'. The
world's attitude to his disciples, he forecasts, will be a con-
tinuation of its attitude to himself—hatred, not love. (In the

Synoptics he sounds a like warning: 'If the master has been called Beelzebub, how much more his household' Matt. 10: 25.) True then, it is true still, and will always be.

If his disciples *belonged to the world*—if they were morally identified with it—*the world* (says Jesus) *would love its own*. As it is, they belong to him—are his chosen friends—and must incur its hostility. Recalling an earlier saying (13: 16), he declares that their friendship with himself will inevitably procure them the world's persecution. It is a case of like master, like disciple. And he traces back (verse 21) the world's hatred of himself and his followers to an ultimate ignorance of God, his Sender.

This ignorance is inexcusable sin. Paul was to teach that the Law of Moses had the effect of throwing men's sin into bold relief. So Jesus here (verse 22) speaks of his own *words*—his own message. *If I had not come* (and 'come' here has the Messianic overtones it has in the phrase 'He that cometh', i.e. the Messiah) *and spoken to them, they would not be guilty of sin; but now they have no excuse for their sin*. From his lips they have had God's offer of salvation, and by their deliberate refusal of it they have condemned themselves. Nor has it been otherwise with his *works*. Pure and unique goodness has been in action among them, and they have culpably rejected it, thus repudiating not himself only but his sender. (Tennyson once said: 'We needs must love the highest when we see it.' But it is not true.) Nonetheless, this hatred of the world is not unforeseen—witness the Jewish scriptures.

But if God has testified to men through the words and works of Jesus, he will continue to testify through the mission of the 'other Paraclete', *the Spirit of truth that issues from the Father*. And Jesus adds: 'You my disciples will, by virtue of your long relation to me, be my witnesses.' Co-witnesses of the Holy Ghost, such is the calling of Christ's disciples, now as then.

20. *Remember what I said*. At 13: 16.

25. *this text in their Law*. Either Ps. 35: 19 or Ps. 69: 4

(*Law* here meaning the whole Old Testament). Jesus calls it *their Law* in order to rivet on the Jews those scriptures on which they so proudly relied.

26. The third 'Paraclete' saying (which resembles the saying about the Spirit in Matt. 10: 20) should be compared with John 14: 16, 26, where the Father sends the Spirit in Christ's name. Needless to say, the precise relations in the Godhead between Father, Son and Spirit are not in question here. All that is said is that the Spirit who witnesses to Christ comes from the Father.

27. *from the first*. From the beginning of Christ's ministry, not from the beginning of the world. Acts 5: 32 also refers to the twofold witness of the Holy Spirit and of the disciples. ✳

THE SPIRIT'S JUDGEMENT OF THE WORLD

'I have told you all this to guard you against the break- **16** down of your faith. They will ban you from the syna- 2 gogue; indeed, the time is coming when anyone who kills you will suppose that he is performing a religious duty. They will do these things because they do not know either 3 the Father or me. I have told you all this so that when the 4 time comes for it to happen you may remember my warning. I did not tell you this at first, because then I was with you; but now I am going away to him who sent me. 5 None of you asks me "Where are you going?" Yet you 6 are plunged into grief because of what I have told you. Nevertheless I tell you the truth: it is for your good that 7 I am leaving you. If I do not go, your Advocate will not come, whereas if I go, I will send him to you. When he 8 comes, he will confute the world, and show where wrong and right and judgement lie. He will convict them of 9 wrong, by their refusal to believe in me; he will convince 10

them that right is on my side, by showing that I go to the
11 Father when I pass from your sight; and he will convince
them of divine judgement, by showing that the Prince of
this world stands condemned.

12   'There is still much that I could say to you, but the
13 burden would be too great for you now. However,
when he comes who is the Spirit of truth, he will guide
you into all the truth; for he will not speak on his own
authority, but will tell only what he hears; and he will
14 make known to you the things that are coming. He will
glorify me, for everything that he makes known to you
15 he will draw from what is mine. All that the Father has
is mine, and that is why I said, "Everything that he makes
known to you he will draw from what is mine."

* There is no real break between chapters 15 and 16. On the
principle of 'forewarned is forearmed', Jesus speaks to his
disciples about their lot in a hostile world (verses 1–7). They
must expect excommunication from the synagogue and indeed
martyrdom at the hands of men who, however well-inten-
tioned, are ignorant of the Father and of himself. In such
bitter times it will be a comfort to recall that Jesus had foretold
it all. There was no need to tell them earlier. But now that he
is going away to his Father, that time has come. The thought
of his departure saddens them ? If only they knew, they would
realize that his going was for their gain. Without it there
could be no helping Holy Spirit.

Then (verse 8) Jesus explains how the Spirit will work on
the conscience of the world, presumably through the inspired preaching of his apostles. The Paraclete's role will be
that of an 'exposer' (see note on verse 8) of sin, and that in
three directions: wrong, right, and judgement.

First, *he will convict them of wrong, by their refusal to believe
in me*. The Spirit will show how sinfully wrong was their

rejection of God's appointed messenger. Second, *he will convince them that right is on my side, by showing that I go to the Father when I pass from your sight.* The Spirit will show that Christ's death was not a criminal's just punishment but a going to the Father who, by receiving him, vindicated the rightness of his cause. Third, *he will convince them of divine judgement, by showing that the Prince of this world stands condemned.* The Spirit will show that Christ's death, apparently a victory for the devil, was really a judgement on him and all his works.

But the Paraclete will do more than expose: he will also *teach* (12 ff.). The Lord's earthly teaching has been incomplete, because it has been limited by his hearers' capacity to understand it. But the Paraclete will guide them into all the truth of Christ's Gospel. (The apostles' teaching and the rest of the New Testament exemplify this Spirit-taught truth.) Like Jesus himself (7: 16, etc.), the Spirit *will tell only what he hears* and he will make known *the things that are coming*—not 'the Last Things' but the events of the New Order to follow on Christ's triumph over death. The Spirit *will glorify me*: will make Christ known in his full majesty, will reveal and irradiate the meaning of his person and work.

1. *to guard you against the breakdown of your faith.* Literally, 'to prevent your being tripped up'. The Greek verb denotes a failure due to obstacles put in the way, contrasted with failure due to disloyalty.

2. *a religious duty.* There was a Jewish maxim, 'Everyone who pours out the blood of the godless is as one who offers a sacrifice'. This was the temper of Saul the persecutor—see Acts 26: 9.

5. *None of you asks me 'Where are you going?'* A good example of the refusal to ask this question today is to be found in those people who say that the crucifix is an adequate symbol of the Christian faith, forgetting that Christ is not on the cross but on the throne.

7. *it is for your good that I am leaving you.* We sometimes envy those who were with Jesus. Yet when the crisis came, the faith

which relied on an external presence went to pieces. A few weeks later, and these same faithless disciples exhibited a strange new boldness and joy in the teeth of persecution. What explains the change? Jesus' promise had come true.

8 ff. *Confute...convict...convince.* The Greek has but one verb here—*elenchō*. It means (1) bring to light; and (2) convict. Now in English the word 'expose' has these same two meanings: (1) display (to the public gaze); and (2) show up. The Paraclete therefore is to be the 'exposer' of the world's sin.

12 f. All revelation is limited by the ability of the receiver to understand it. Here we find the idea of progressive revelation. When it is said that the Paraclete *will guide...into all the truth*, the thought is not of further new truth but of the whole truth set forth by the incarnate Son of God. What are *the things that are coming*? Not the Last Things (secrets revealed at the end of the world) but 'the spiritual Kingdom which should come such as the apostles saw shortly after his Resurrection' (Calvin). ✳

VICTORY OVER THE WORLD

16 'A little while, and you see me no more; again a little
17 while, and you will see me.' Some of his disciples said to one another, 'What does he mean by this: "A little while, and you will not see me, and again a little while, and you will see me", and by this: "Because I am going to my
18 Father"?' So they asked, 'What is this "little while" that he speaks of? We do not know what he means.'

19 Jesus knew that they were wanting to question him, and said, 'Are you discussing what I said: "A little while, and you will not see me, and again a little while, and you
20 will see me"? In very truth I tell you, you will weep and mourn, but the world will be glad. But though you will

be plunged in grief, your grief will be turned to joy. A 21
woman in labour is in pain because her time has come; but
when the child is born she forgets the anguish in her joy
that a man has been born into the world. So it is with you: 22
for the moment you are sad at heart; but I shall see you
again, and then you will be joyful, and no one shall rob
you of your joy. When that day comes you will ask 23
nothing of me. In very truth I tell you, if you ask the
Father for anything in my name, he will give it you. So 24
far you have asked nothing in my name. Ask and you will
receive, that your joy may be complete.

'Till now I have been using figures of speech; a time is 25
coming when I shall no longer use figures, but tell you of
the Father in plain words. When that day comes you will 26
make your request in my name, and I do not say that I shall
pray to the Father for you, for the Father loves you him- 27
self, because you have loved me and believed that I came
from God. I came from the Father and have come into 28
the world. Now I am leaving the world again and going
to the Father.' His disciples said, 'Why, this is plain speak- 29
ing; this is no figure of speech. We are certain now that 30
you know everything, and do not need to be questioned;
because of this we believe that you have come from
God.'

Jesus answered, 'Do you now believe? Look, the hour 31,32
is coming, has indeed already come, when you are all to
be scattered, each to his home, leaving me alone. Yet I am
not alone, because the Father is with me. I have told you 33
all this so that in me you may find peace. In the world you
will have trouble. But courage! The victory is mine; I
have conquered the world.'

✻ To the promise of the Paraclete Jesus adds another, that of his own return from death in *a little while* (the equivalent in this Gospel of the 'after three days' in the earlier tradition). But how to 'square' this quick return with his declared journey to the Father is the disciples' difficulty. Will not his return take longer? Jesus replies (19 ff.) that, though a time of grief awaits them, the end, like that of a woman's labour, will be sorrow-forgetting joy, a joy at the sight of their returning Lord which none will be able to destroy. The little parable of the woman in labour (verse 21) is not just a familiar illustration of how sorrow is often the prelude to joy. Its key is to be found in Isa. 66: 7–9, 14 where the prophet compares the Messianic salvation which relieves the affliction of God's people to a woman's joy in childbirth. (The reader should look the passage up.) In other words, the death and resurrection of the Lord is seen as a final and decisive act of God. In *that day* (verse 23), i.e. of the Resurrection and the coming of the Spirit, the disciples will bring their requests not to Jesus but to the Father, and in the great reunion of the Son with the Father in heaven they will gain a new idea of the power of prayer and of the place of Christ in their devotions when praying to the Father. To act on this discovery will be to taste a *joy* never known before.

Figurative speech, he says (25 ff.), has played a large part in his mission now ending; but hereafter such veiled speech will yield to *plain words*. *When that day comes*, they will ask God for what they need in Christ's name, and he will not need to ask the Father on their behalf. Their communion will be direct with the Father, a Father loving them for their love of his Son and their belief in him. Then (verse 28), in four brief phrases, Jesus declares his origin and destiny. As once he left the Father to enter the world, so now he leaves it to go to the Father. *Why, this is plain speaking*, say the disciples. Sure now of his divine mission, they feel no need for further questions.

Thereupon (verse 31) Jesus shatters their confidence with the warning that very soon they will be *scattered* and *leave* him *alone.* (We remember that the grain of wheat must die alone if it is to bear a rich harvest.) Yet, deserted by men, he is *not alone,* for he has the Father's companionship. Such has always been his teaching, its purpose to give them peace not in themselves but in himself. In their dealings with the world they will encounter opposition. But—and these are his last words —*courage! The victory is mine; I have conquered the world.* He speaks as if the cross were already behind him—that cross in which he conquers the world by redeeming it and by defeating its diabolical ruler.

20. *your grief will be turned to joy.* See 20: 20.

22. *no one shall rob you of your joy.* The true joy of Easter, once experienced, can never be forgotten. In face of all doubters it cries, 'I know that my Redeemer liveth'.

23. *you will ask nothing of me.* It is possible also to translate the Greek, 'You will ask me no questions' (so the R.S.V., Moffatt, etc.). That is, they will not need to question Jesus as they had been doing, for they will have the Holy Spirit to guide them into all the truth. But there is no reference to the Holy Spirit in the immediate context. Moreover, the emphatic place of *me* in the original Greek is a strong argument for the N.E.B. text.

24. *Ask and you will receive.* Matt. 7: 7; Luke 11: 9.

31 f. *you are all to be scattered.* The same verb is used in Mark 14: 27, by Jesus as he moves, with the disciples, to the Mount of Olives from the upper room.

32. *I am not alone.* 'At every stage of his departure to the Father, the Father is with him, even as at every stage of our pilgrimage to our Father's house we are at home with the Father' (Temple).

33. *The victory is mine; I have conquered the world.* Paul too declared that in the cross Christ triumphed over the powers of evil (Col. 2: 15), and speaking of Christ's resurrection and all that it meant, said, 'God be praised, he gives us the victory through our Lord Jesus Christ' (1 Cor. 15: 57).

As the first instruction ended with a summons to advance

against the enemy (14: 31), the second ends with the announcement of victory. Both are on the inward, spiritual plane. In
what follows, they will be fulfilled in action. *

THE GREAT PRAYER

* Before leaving the upper room—or perhaps somewhere on
the way to Gethsemane—Jesus offers what is traditionally
known as the High-Priestly Prayer. As the High Priest on the
Day of Atonement, the great annual feast of the Jews (see
Lev. 16), prayed for himself, for the priests and Levites, and
for the whole congregation of Israel, so now Jesus prays for
himself, for the disciples, and for all future believers. It is
the record of Jesus' self-consecration as it lived in the memory
of his intimate disciple, and it falls into three parts:

(*a*) The Son and the Father (verses 1–8).
(*b*) The Son and the disciples (verses 9–19).
(*c*) The Son, the disciples and the world (verses 20–6). *

THE SON AND THE FATHER

17 After these words Jesus looked up to heaven and said:
    'Father, the hour has come. Glorify thy Son, that the
2 Son may glorify thee. For thou hast made him sovereign
over all mankind, to give eternal life to all whom thou
3 hast given him. This is eternal life: to know thee who
alone art truly God, and Jesus Christ whom thou hast sent.
4   'I have glorified thee on earth by completing the work
5 which thou gavest me to do; and now, Father, glorify me
in thine own presence with the glory which I had with
thee before the world began.
6   'I have made thy name known to the men whom thou
didst give me out of the world. They were thine, thou

gavest them to me, and they have obeyed thy command. Now they know that all thy gifts have come to me from 7 thee; for I have taught them all that I learned from thee, 8 and they have received it: they know with certainty that I came from thee; they have had faith to believe that thou didst send me.

✶ The long-awaited hour—*the hour* of his death in which God's glory is to be supremely revealed—*has* now *come*: and Jesus stands with his disciples in the presence of the *Father*. (His prayer in Aramaic would begin *Abba*. Cf. Mark 14: 36.)

He begins by recalling the commission the Father has given him—*to give eternal life to all*—and reporting that he has carried it out (verse 4), prays for *the glory* which he had in heaven with the Father before he relinquished it for his earthly ministry. Then (verses 6–8) he renders to God an account of his steward- ship. To the men God gave him he has made God's *name known*, i.e. revealed his fatherly nature and purpose; and they have responded with obedience, so that they now *know with certainty* that their master is from God.

1. *Glorify thy Son, that the Son may glorify thee.* The Father glorifies his Son by sustaining him in his perfect obedience, as the Son glorifies the Father by the perfect obedience he offers.

3. This sentence, as it were in brackets, is the evangelist's comment, and his only attempt at a definition of that eternal life which is the main theme of his Gospel. It consists, he says, in a growing acquaintance with the only true ʾGod through the Messiah, his messenger to men. Knowledge of God does not mean theological erudition. It means personal communion—an 'I–thou' encounter—with God, such as is described, for example, in Ps. 139. Nor is John speaking of a *double* knowledge here, as though one began with the know- ledge of the true God and then went on to gain knowledge of Christ. It is *one* knowledge of God—one fellowship with him—that which comes through Christ. ✶

THE SON AND THE DISCIPLES

9 'I pray for them; I am not praying for the world but for those whom thou hast given me, because they belong to
10 thee. All that is mine is thine, and what is thine is mine; and through them has my glory shone.

11   'I am to stay no longer in the world, but they are still in the world, and I am on my way to thee. Holy Father, protect by the power of thy name those whom thou hast
12 given me, that they may be one, as we are one. When I was with them, I protected by the power of thy name those whom thou hast given me, and kept them safe. Not one of them is lost except the man who must be lost, for Scripture has to be fulfilled.

13   'And now I am coming to thee; but while I am still in the world I speak these words, so that they may have my
14 joy within them in full measure. I have delivered thy word to them, and the world hates them because they are
15 strangers in the world, as I am. I pray thee, not to take them out of the world, but to keep them from the evil one.
16, 17 They are strangers in the world, as I am. Consecrate them
18 by the truth; thy word is truth. As thou hast sent me into
19 the world, I have sent them into the world, and for their sake I now consecrate myself, that they too may be consecrated by the truth.

✻ Jesus now intercedes for his disciples.

I pray for them; I am not praying for the world. This does not mean that the world is 'past praying for', as the saying goes. Are we not told that 'God loved the world so much that he gave his only Son' to save it? It means that the world's only hope is that it should cease being 'the world' and become,

like the disciples, the property of God and his Christ (Rev.
11: 15).

The prayer that follows has four petitions. First (verse 11),
Jesus prays that the *Holy Father* will *protect* the disciples by his
gracious providence (*the power of thy name*), so *that they may
be one, as we are one*: one, like Father and Son, in heart
and purpose; for, lacking this unity, their mission must fail.
During his own ministry he has kept his disciples safe, losing only
'the man of wasted life'—or, as the N.E.B. renders, *the man
who must be lost*, as scripture said. Second (verse 13), he prays
that they may fully know the *joy*—the joy of accomplished
work—which has been his. This will compensate for the
world's hatred which will surely be theirs for their loyalty to
Christ. Third (verse 15), he prays that, even while exposed
to the perils of living in the *world*, they may be kept *from the
evil one*. (Here surely we have the language of the Lord's
Prayer.) Lastly (verse 17), he prays God to *consecrate them by
the truth*. Consecration here means being equipped, or made
fit, for divine service. This will be theirs as they are brought
into *the truth* which is the *word*, or revelation, of God (Ps. 119:
114). So they will be fitted for the work to which he is now
sending them.

But, as verse 19 shows, consecration involves more than
this. *Consecrate*, a sacrificial term, means to set apart for a
holy purpose what is flawless. And when Jesus says, *for their
sake I now consecrate myself*, he is referring to the offering of his
own sinless life to God on the cross. This offering, he says, is
for their sake . . . that they too may be consecrated by the truth (or
better, 'truly consecrated'), i.e. that they may be fit to serve
God as truly dedicated men.

12. *the man who must be lost.* He who complained about
waste (Mark 14: 4; John 12: 4) was 'the one waste product' of
Christ's ministry.

19. *for their sake I now consecrate myself.* Nowadays we talk
much about self-consecration, or dedication, as if by our own
efforts we could make ourselves worth a holy God's having.

This is not the view of the New Testament, or of this passage. They teach that we are not worthy to consecrate ourselves till we have been consecrated by God in Christ—consecrated by sharing in the grace of the hallowing cross. ✳

THE SON, THE DISCIPLES AND THE WORLD

20 'But it is not for these alone that I pray, but for those also
21 who through their words put their faith in me; may they all be one: as thou, Father, art in me, and I in thee, so also may they be in us, that the world may believe that thou
22 didst send me. The glory which thou gavest me I have
23 given to them, that they may be one, as we are one; I in them and thou in me, may they be perfectly one. Then the world will learn that thou didst send me, that thou didst love them as thou didst me.

24 'Father, I desire that these men, who are thy gift to me, may be with me where I am, so that they may look upon my glory, which thou hast given me because thou didst
25 love me before the world began. O righteous Father, although the world does not know thee, I know thee, and
26 these men know that thou didst send me. I made thy name known to them, and will make it known, so that the love thou hadst for me may be in them, and I may be in them.'

✳ The third part of the prayer reaches out to embrace all who, through the apostles' preaching, will confess their faith in Christ. It is a prayer for their unity: *may they all be one.* But how?

as thou, Father, art in me, and I in thee. It is to find its ideal in the unity between Father and Son—in a personal relationship of mutual love, not in some external incorporation. Such unity among his believers, says Jesus, will convince the world of his divine mission.

As if it had already happened, Jesus declares (verse 22) that he has given the Church *the glory*—that of the incarnate ministry—God had given him, to the same great end, that they may be *perfectly one*. So the world will learn that Jesus is God's true Messenger and be sure of God's love for them.

Again, invoking God as *Father* (verse 24), Jesus now prays that those who have formed his Father's gift to him, *may be with me where I am*, to see his God-given glory. It is 'a prayer that the Church Militant may become the Church Triumphant', and *my glory* here means Christ's glory within the Godhead.

The last two verses (25 f.) review Jesus' whole mission among men. Coming to a world with a knowledge (his own unique knowledge of God) which it lacked, he has revealed God's *name*—his nature—to men, and will continue to do so. How and when? By the cross, say some commentators. By the Spirit, say others. Why not both? And the whole purpose of this revelation is that the Father's love for Christ the Son may indwell the disciples. So the final vision is of a group of men who love God and love one another. ✳

The Final Conflict

THE ARREST

AFTER THESE WORDS, Jesus went out with his disciples, **18** and crossed the Kedron ravine. There was a garden there, and he and his disciples went into it. The place was 2 known to Judas, his betrayer, because Jesus had often met there with his disciples. So Judas took a detachment of 3 soldiers, and police provided by the chief priests and the

Pharisees, equipped with lanterns, torches, and weapons,
4 and made his way to the garden. Jesus, knowing all that
was coming upon him, went out to them and asked,
5 'Who is it you want?' 'Jesus of Nazareth', they answered.
Jesus said, 'I am he.' And there stood Judas the traitor
6 with them. When he said, 'I am he', they drew back and
7 fell to the ground. Again Jesus asked, 'Who is it you
8 want?' 'Jesus of Nazareth', they answered. Then Jesus
said, 'I have told you that I am he. If I am the man you
9 want, let these others go.' (This was to make good his
words, 'I have not lost one of those whom thou gavest
10 me.') Thereupon Simon Peter drew the sword he was
wearing and struck at the High Priest's servant, cutting
11 off his right ear. (The servant's name was Malchus.) Jesus
said to Peter, 'Sheathe your sword. This is the cup my
Father has given me; shall I not drink it?'

✳ A comparison with the earlier tradition (Mark 14: 32–52)
will show that, as usual, John goes his own way. He does not
mention the Judas kiss, and there is but one echo (verse 11) of
the Agony. But he names the ravine and the smiter and the
smitten in the garden clash, and includes Roman soldiers
among the arresting party.

In John's narrative, Jesus goes voluntarily, open-eyed, even
majestically, to the cross.

1. *went out*: of the city, as *crossed the Kedron ravine* implies.
Kedron (2 Sam. 15: 23), dry in summer but a torrent in winter,
separates the Mount of Olives from the Temple Mount. The
garden is Gethsemane.

3. *a detachment of soldiers*. Roman auxiliaries. Since the
Jews represented Jesus' influence over the people as a public
menace, the Romans probably lent troops to assist the Jewish
police in quelling any possible disturbance during the arrest.

5. *I am he*, i.e. the man you want. With this word Jesus

must have stepped out of the darkness into the light of the torches.

6. The arresting party recoiled before the moral ascendancy of Jesus.

8. *let these others go.* 'The Shepherd went to meet the wolf to save his flock' (Dodd). Cf. 10: 15.

9. Refers back to 17: 12.

10. An ineffectual attempt at resistance to arrest. For the disciples' swords see Luke 22: 38. Luke 22: 50 also mentions the servant's *right ear*.

11. Matt. 26: 52 preserves a slightly different version of the saying about sheathing the sword.

the cup (Mark 10: 38 and 14: 36) is, as often in the Old Testament, a metaphor for divinely appointed suffering: 'Shall I refuse the lot appointed me by my Father?' ✵

THE PRELIMINARY EXAMINATION: PETER'S DENIAL

The troops with their commander, and the Jewish police, 12 now arrested Jesus and secured him. They took him first 13 to Annas. Annas was father-in-law of Caiaphas, the High Priest for that year—the same Caiaphas who had advised 14 the Jews that it would be to their interest if one man died for the whole people. Jesus was followed by Simon Peter 15 and another disciple. This disciple, who was acquainted with the High Priest, went with Jesus into the High Priest's courtyard, but Peter halted at the door outside. So the 16 other disciple, the High Priest's acquaintance, went out again and spoke to the woman at the door, and brought Peter in. The maid on duty at the door said to Peter, 'Are 17 you another of this man's disciples?' 'I am not', he said. The servants and the police had made a charcoal fire, be- 18 cause it was cold, and were standing round it warming themselves. And Peter too was standing with them, sharing the warmth.

19 The High Priest questioned Jesus about his disciples and
20 about what he taught. Jesus replied, 'I have spoken openly to all the world; I have always taught in synagogue and in the temple, where all Jews congregate; I have said nothing
21 in secret. Why question me? Ask my hearers what I told
22 them; they know what I said.' When he said this, one of the police struck him on the face, exclaiming, 'Is that the
23 way to answer the High Priest?' Jesus replied, 'If I spoke amiss, state it in evidence; if I spoke well, why strike me?'
24 So Annas sent him bound to Caiaphas the High Priest.
25 Meanwhile Peter stood warming himself. The others asked, 'Are you another of his disciples?' But he denied
26 it: 'I am not', he said. One of the High Priest's servants, a relation of the man whose ear Peter had cut off, insisted,
27 'Did I not see you with him in the garden?' Peter denied again; and just then a cock crew.

* All the evangelists agree that there was (*a*) an ecclesiastical trial, and (*b*) a civil trial. But there are differences among the evangelists in their records of both events. Suffice it here to say that the amount of verbal resemblance between John and the Synoptists, in the Trial as well as in the whole Passion story, is almost the minimum if the same story is to be told at all. Here as elsewhere we believe John was drawing on his own independent sources of tradition.

After the arrest Jesus is taken first, for preliminary examination, before Annas, father-in-law of Caiaphas, the actual High Priest for that year (cf. 11: 51). (Though John is our only authority for this private and informal inquiry, we need not doubt that it happened.) In the rear follow Peter and *another disciple*—possibly the Beloved Disciple, though we cannot be certain. The latter, because he is known to the High Priest, is allowed into the High Priest's courtyard at once. But Peter is kept waiting outside until his companion speaks a word to *the woman at the door*. The portress, in some doubt, asks him if he is a follower of Jesus. His denial gains him admission, and he merges in the crowd of shivering servants round a glowing charcoal fire. (John's note about the *other disciple*—not in the Synoptics—explains how Peter got into the courtyard at all, as Mark 14: 54 records.)

Then *the High Priest* (a title not confined to the actual reigning High Priest—see Luke 3: 2 and Acts 4: 6) questions Jesus about his disciples and his teaching. He is preparing the ground for a political charge before Pilate, and would like to extort evidence that Jesus, by training a band of rebels, is guilty of sedition. Jesus repudiates the charge—he has always taught in public, never conspired in secret (cf. Mark 14: 49). At this one of the Jewish police, thinking his answer insolent, strikes Jesus on the face. Those who wish to take Jesus' teaching in Matt. 5: 39 quite literally should ponder the fact that, when Jesus was himself struck on the face, he made a dignified remonstrance and did not merely 'turn the other cheek'. When Annas fails to extract the desired answer, he sends Jesus *bound* to his son-in-law, *Caiaphas*, the official *High Priest*.

Possibly, as Jesus passed through the courtyard, the servants saw him, so that Peter was again questioned—this time by some servants. Again he denied all connexion with Jesus. But the third question, put by a kinsman of the wounded Malchus, was more dangerous; and he was glad to deny it outright. The time was about 3 a.m.

27. *just then a cock crew*. What Peter heard was probably not a rooster but a bugle-note (*gallicinium*) from the Fortress Antonia at the close of the third watch (12 midnight to 3 a.m.), announcing the changing of the guard. 'Cockcrow' was the name of the third of the four Roman watches in the night. ✱

THE TRIAL BEFORE PILATE

28 From Caiaphas Jesus was led into the Governor's headquarters. It was now early morning, and the Jews themselves stayed outside the headquarters to avoid defilement,
29 so that they could eat the Passover meal. So Pilate went
out to them and asked, 'What charge do you bring against
30 this man?' 'If he were not a criminal,' they replied,
31 'we should not have brought him before you.' Pilate
said, 'Take him away and try him by your own
law.' The Jews answered, 'We are not allowed to put
32 any man to death.' Thus they ensured the fulfilment of
the words by which Jesus had indicated the manner of
his death.

33　Pilate then went back into his headquarters and summoned Jesus. 'Are you the king of the Jews?' he asked.
34 Jesus said, 'Is that your own idea, or have others suggested
35 it to you?' 'What! am I a Jew?' said Pilate. 'Your own
nation and their chief priests have brought you before me.
36 What have you done?' Jesus replied, 'My kingdom does
not belong to this world. If it did, my followers would
be fighting to save me from arrest by the Jews. My
37 kingly authority comes from elsewhere.' 'You are a king,
then?' said Pilate. Jesus answered, '"King" is your word.
My task is to bear witness to the truth. For this was I
born; for this I came into the world, and all who are not
38 deaf to truth listen to my voice.' Pilate said, 'What is
truth?', and with those words went out again to the Jews.
39 'For my part,' he said, 'I find no case against him. But
you have a custom that I release one prisoner for you at
Passover. Would you like me to release the king of the

Jews?' Again the clamour rose: 'Not him; we want 40 Barabbas!' (Barabbas was a bandit.)

* John's account of this trial is probably independent of the earlier evangelists. But the main features—Pilate's reluctance to condemn, the Passover custom of releasing a prisoner, Barabbas, the scourging and mocking, and Pilate's final capitulation to the Jews' demand for crucifixion—naturally occur in both John and Mark. More clearly than the earlier evangelists John brings out the theological issues. We should also note that the Trial, as he narrates it, falls into a series of scenes, alternatively outside and inside the Governor's headquarters.

In the *early morning* (before 6 a.m.) Jesus is taken from Caiaphas to Pilate's *headquarters* in the Fortress Antonia—as many believe—the Jews staying outside to avoid ritual defilement in an 'unclean' place. When Pilate suggests that this is a case for the Jews themselves to try, they reply that they have no power to execute a criminal (see note on verse 31).

Returning inside his headquarters (verse 33), Pilate privately examines Jesus. He knows that the real charge is sedition; but Jesus does not look like a rival to the Emperor. Hence his question: *Are you the king of the Jews?* Jesus replies in effect, 'Is this your own honest question, or are you merely a tool in the hands of the Jews?' When Pilate answers, 'It is these Jews, your own people, who have put you here. What is your real offence?' Jesus' answer takes up the real charge—that of being a king. Kingship—as the world understands the word—he disavows. If his kingship were political, his supporters would be found fighting for him now. But, he says, *my kingly authority comes from elsewhere* (verse 36).

'So, you are a king?' retorts Pilate. Jesus' reply, '"*King*" *is your word*', is neither clear yes nor clear no, but an assent given as concession. The phrase, if misleading, has truth in it. For, as he goes on to say, if he is a king, it is in a higher realm. He has come *to bear witness to the truth*, i.e. not to assert his own sovereignty but to reveal God whose kingdom is the truth faintly suggested by every earthly kingdom.

All this, however, is over pagan Pilate's head. *What is truth?* he says, wearily. Not 'jesting Pilate' (as Bacon said) but cynical Pilate, the man of the world, who has presided at so very many trials and knows how hard it is to decide on which side truth lies.

And again (verse 38) he goes outside to the waiting Jews. Declaring that he finds *no case* against Jesus, he now tries to persuade them to accept a compromise—formal condemnation and release according to a Passover custom. But *again the clamour rose: 'Not him; we want Barabbas!'* Barabbas was a criminal, but he had defied hated Rome (Mark 15: 7); and the crowd preferred this gangster-patriot to one who had so sadly disappointed their nationalist aspirations. *Barabbas was a bandit* is one of John's brief but dramatic asides (cf. 13: 30). The choice was no accident: it was a symbol. Invited to choose between its real king and a bandit, the crowd (shall we say the world?) chose the *bandit*.

28. *the Governor's headquarters.* Formerly it was supposed that these were in Herod's palace in the west of the city. Recent discoveries by L. H. Vincent make it probable that they were in the Fortress Antonia, north-west of the Temple.

so that they could eat the Passover meal. The Last Supper, then, can hardly have been a *regular* Passover.

31. *We are not allowed to put any man to death.* The truth of this statement was contested some decades ago by the German scholar Lietzmann. He argued that, under the Roman Empire, the Sanhedrin had the right to carry out capital sentences. In *The Trial of Jesus* (1953), G. D. Kilpatrick not only shows his evidence to be rickety but invokes in John's favour the testimony of both the Palestinian Talmud and the historian Josephus.

39. *a custom.* Cf. Mark 16: 6. For this we have no Palestinian parallel; but a papyrus of A.D. 85 describes a trial before an Egyptian governor (Septimius) who says to the prisoner,

'Thou art worthy of scourging...but I will give thee to the people'. ✻

Pilate now took Jesus and had him flogged; and the **19** 1, 2 soldiers plaited a crown of thorns and placed it on his head, and robed him in a purple cloak. Then time after 3 time they came up to him, crying, 'Hail, King of the Jews!', and struck him on the face.

Once more Pilate came out and said to the Jews, 'Here 4 he is; I am bringing him out to let you know that I find no case against him'; and Jesus came out, wearing the 5 crown of thorns and the purple cloak. 'Behold the Man!' said Pilate. The chief priests and their henchmen saw him 6 and shouted, 'Crucify! crucify!' 'Take him and crucify him yourselves,' said Pilate; 'for my part I find no case against him.' The Jews answered, 'We have a law; and 7 by that law he ought to die, because he has claimed to be Son of God.'

When Pilate heard that, he was more afraid than ever, 8 and going back into his headquarters he asked Jesus, 9 'Where have you come from?' But Jesus gave him no answer. 'Do you refuse to speak to me?' said Pilate. 10 'Surely you know that I have authority to release you, and I have authority to crucify you?' 'You would have 11 no authority at all over me', Jesus replied, 'if it had not been granted you from above; and therefore the deeper guilt lies with the man who handed me over to you.'

From that moment Pilate tried hard to release him; but 12 the Jews kept shouting, 'If you let this man go, you are no friend to Caesar; any man who claims to be a king is defying Caesar.' When Pilate heard what they were say- 13

ing, he brought Jesus out and took his seat on the tribunal
at the place known as 'The Pavement' ('Gabbatha' in the
14 language of the Jews). It was the eve of Passover, about
15 noon. Pilate said to the Jews, 'Here is your king.' They
shouted, 'Away with him! Away with him! Crucify
him!' 'Crucify your king?' said Pilate. 'We have no king
16 but Caesar', the Jews replied. Then at last, to satisfy them,
he handed Jesus over to be crucified.

✳ Again, John seems to owe nothing to the earlier evangelists.

Pilate now took Jesus and had him flogged. This was the Roman
method of examining an alien or a slave—not a punishment,
but a means of finding out the truth or extracting a confession.
Probably he hoped that the Jews, content with scourging,
would not insist on crucifixion. To the official scourging the
soldiers added mock coronation, the thorny crown to parody
the Emperor's laurel-wreath, a legionary's scarlet cloak to
simulate the Emperor's purple robes. The salutation *Hail, King
of the Jews!* suggests that the charge brought by the Sanhedrin
to Pilate was that Jesus claimed to be the Messiah, i.e. the King
of the Jews. Cf. Mark 14: 61 f.

Outside headquarters again (verse 4), Pilate declares the
prisoner innocent and exhibits him, crowned and bleeding,
to the Jews, hoping to move their pity. *Behold the Man!* On
Pilate's lips, words half pitying, half contemptuous: but, by
unconscious irony, how much more: 'the Man, the Son of
Man, the Man from heaven' (3: 13). When *the chief priests*
and their supporters persist in their demand for crucifixion,
exasperated Pilate dares them to take the law into their own
hands. Then the Jews blurt out their original charge—blasphemy, a sin punishable by death (Lev. 24: 16): *he has claimed
to be Son of God.* Cf. 5: 18; 10: 33.

Growing afraid (verse 8), Pilate next questions Jesus about
his origin, but gets no answer. There was an answer to the
question; but how could Pilate be expected to understand?

Besides, Jesus was moving to a predetermined end, and he knew it. Grimly Pilate reminds him that he has *authority*—from Caesar—to spare or to execute. Jesus' reply is that Caesar's authority comes from God (cf. Rom. 13: 1): *You would have no authority at all over me, if it had not been granted you from above.* Pilate's competence to order the execution of the Son of God is derived from God himself! When Jesus adds, *the deeper guilt lies with the man who handed me over to you,* he means Caiaphas, not Judas. The guilt of Caiaphas is greater than Pilate's because he is deliberately using his God-given authority to further his own wicked ends.

Pilate is still set on releasing Jesus (verse 12), but the Jews' veiled threat to send a damaging report about him to Caesar worries him. Taking his seat *about noon* on the portable platform or *tribunal at the place known as 'The Pavement'* (see note on verse 13), he again exhibits Jesus to the crowd: *Here is your king!* only to evoke from them a savage demand for immediate crucifixion.

Crucify your king? (verse 15). The question—a flash of irritable sarcasm—is Pilate's last feeble attempt to stay them from their course. *We have no king but Caesar,* they reply. It is the Jews' final desertion of God. They had claimed that God was their only king. Having extracted this avowal of loyalty to Caesar, Pilate, *to satisfy them, handed Jesus over to be crucified.*

1. According to Mark and Matthew, the scourging apparently took place after sentence had been passed. According to Luke 23: 16, Pilate made the suggestion 'I will scourge him and let him go'. In John the scourging is part of the examination of the prisoner, a Roman legal device to extract evidence or obtain a confession. There is an excellent parallel in Acts 22: 24. May not John be right on this point—unless we are prepared to believe that Jesus was twice scourged? Pilate's act may then be taken as an attempt at compromise, to placate the Jews.

13. *took his seat on the tribunal.* Some have taken the Greek verb transitively and translated: 'he [Pilate] seated him [Jesus]

on the tribunal', i.e. Pilate enthroned him, in a piece of ironical buffoonery. This interpretation is dramatic, but is hardly history. Fear, not mockery, was the uppermost element in Pilate's mood. '*The Pavement*' ('*Gabbatha*' *in the language of the Jews*), thanks to the researches of L. H. Vincent, we now know to have been in the court of the Antonia. Covering 2500 square metres, it stood on a rocky elevation to which the Aramaic *Gabbatha*, 'ridge' was properly applied.

14. *It was the eve of Passover, about noon.* According to Mark 15: 25, the hour of the crucifixion was 9 a.m. According to John it was *about noon* that Pilate passed sentence. Nobody has yet cleared up this discrepancy. Those interested will find a good discussion in Sir William Ramsay's article in *Hastings' Dictionary of the Bible*, vol. 5, 477-9. The discrepancy, he says, springs from the ancients' carelessness in measuring time. We must not think that, with the passage of the years, memory became obscured. If we could consult various contemporary statements, we should find the difference already there. Who then is likelier to be right? Ramsay bids us follow John who, as 1: 39; 4: 6; 4: 52 show, is careful to record precise hours, probably because he was using the record of an eyewitness (19: 35). ✲

THE CRUCIFIXION

17 Jesus was now taken in charge and, carrying his own cross, went out to the Place of the Skull, as it is called (or,
18 in the Jews' language, 'Golgotha'), where they crucified him, and with him two others, one on the right, one on the left, and Jesus between them.

19 And Pilate wrote an inscription to be fastened to the
20 cross; it read, 'Jesus of Nazareth King of the Jews.' This inscription was read by many Jews, because the place where Jesus was crucified was not far from the city, and

the inscription was in Hebrew, Latin, and Greek. Then 21
the Jewish chief priests said to Pilate, 'You should not
write "King of the Jews"; write, "He claimed to be king
of the Jews."' Pilate replied, 'What I have written, I have 22
written.'

The soldiers, having crucified Jesus, took possession of 23
his clothes, and divided them into four parts, one for each
soldier, leaving out the tunic. The tunic was seamless,
woven in one piece throughout; so they said to one 24
another, 'We must not tear this; let us toss for it'; and
thus the text of Scripture came true: 'They shared my
garments among them, and cast lots for my clothing.'

That is what the soldiers did. But meanwhile near the 25
cross where Jesus hung stood his mother, with her sister,
Mary wife of Clopas, and Mary of Magdala. Jesus saw 26
his mother, with the disciple whom he loved standing
beside her. He said to her, 'Mother, there is your son';
and to the disciple, 'There is your mother'; and from 27
that moment the disciple took her into his home.

After that, Jesus, aware that all had now come to its 28
appointed end, said in fulfilment of Scripture, 'I thirst.'
A jar stood there full of sour wine; so they soaked a 29
sponge with the wine, fixed it on a javelin, and held it up
to his lips. Having received the wine, he said, 'It is 30
accomplished!' He bowed his head and gave up his
spirit.

✻ In the Crucifixion story John, as usual, goes his own way.
Thus, at the beginning, we learn that Jesus, *carrying his own
cross*, went out to Golgotha. Cf. Mark 15: 21. It is natural to
reconcile the two accounts by supposing that Jesus set out
carrying his own cross (or rather the cross-piece) and that,

when he sank under its weight, the Romans commandeered
Simon of Cyrene to carry it. *The Place of the Skull* (Hebrew:
Golgotha; Latin: *Calvaria*), to which the execution party took
him, was probably hard by the present Church of the Holy
Sepulchre. The two malefactors between whom he was cruci-
fied may well have been supporters of Barabbas.

It was the custom to fasten to the cross a *titulus*, i.e. a white
board inscribed with the name and the offence of the criminal.
That *Pilate wrote* it means that some underling did the job
for him; but the actual inscription (whose wording varies
slightly in the four Gospels) was doubtless of his suggesting.
We need not be surprised that it was trilingual—'polyglot
notices in the Hellenistic age were probably almost as common
as they are in continental railway carriages today' (Barrett);
yet it stands as an unconscious prophecy of Jesus' universal
Kingship. Of course the Jews objected to the wording—in
their eyes Jesus was 'the Great Pretender'; and Pilate's famous
refusal to alter it suggests the obstinacy of a weak man who
has given in on the main issue.

A crucified man's clothes were the perquisites of his execu-
tioners, who in this case formed a quaternion, or group of
four. But when they set about dividing Christ's garments into
four lots, they left out the tunic, noting that it was *seamless*,
and decided to *toss for it* instead. The fact that the High-Priest's
robe was also seamless has led the ingenious to find here a
symbol of the Church's indivisibility. We prefer to accept the
statement as one of fact, and not to speculate. Here (cf. Mark
15: 24) the evangelist notes the fulfilment of Ps. 22: 18, 'the
Psalm of the Suffering Servant', so often quoted in the New
Testament that it clearly served the early Christians as a source
for 'testimonies' to Christ's Passion.

The Synoptics record the presence of women at the Crucifixion, 'watching from a distance' (Mark 15: 40), though they
do not name Jesus' mother. John mentions her along with
three others.

The next episode of the *sour wine* should not be confused

with Jesus' refusal of the *drugged* wine (Mark 15: 36). This sour wine was the usual drink of the soldiery. When Jesus had drunk the sour wine, he cried 'It is accomplished!'. If we recall 4: 34 and 17: 4, this can only be a shout of triumph: 'I have finished the work my Father gave me to do.' The Good Shepherd has laid down his life for the sheep (10: 17 f.). The Lamb of God has borne the sins of the world.

Then *he bowed his head and gave up his spirit*—surrendered it to his Father, as in Luke 23: 46 (but see note on verse 30).

17. 'Gordon's Calvary', a skull-shaped hillock outside the modern city's northern wall, has lost favour with the experts who now increasingly favour the traditional site at the Church of the Holy Sepulchre.

25 ff. Probably four women are meant: Jesus' mother, her sister, Mary wife of Clopas, and Mary Magdalene. From Mark 15: 40 and Matt. 27: 56 we learn that Mary Magdalene, Mary the mother of James and Joseph, and Salome the mother of the sons of Zebedee were present. If identification of these lists is allowable, Salome was the sister of Mary, the Lord's mother, and Christ's commendation of his mother to John becomes intelligible. But did he really do so? Some have doubted it—unwarrantably, we think. Surely it does not strain faith to believe that Jesus, as head of the family, should have made such provision for his mother and entrusted her to the Beloved Disciple rather than to his unbelieving brethren?

29. 'On a hyssop' is the reading of all the MSS save one. But hyssop, a small wall-growing plant, is ill-adapted to raise a sponge to the lips of a crucified man (Mark 15: 36 speaks of a 'reed' or 'cane'). Long ago an old scholar, Camerarius, suggested that the letters *op* had been mistakenly repeated and that for *hussōpō* 'on hyssop' we should read *hussō* 'on a javelin'. This reading has turned up in a recently discovered MS and the N.E.B. translators have rightly accepted it.

30. *It is accomplished!* Since the verb was sometimes used of completing a religious rite or sacrifice, the meaning is possibly, 'The sacrifice is complete!' Cf. 17: 19.

gave up his spirit. Hoskyns, pointing to 7: 39, suggests that we should here spell *spirit* with a capital S. On the cross Jesus 'handed over the Spirit' to his followers. Not only is this super-subtle, but it contradicts 20: 23, where John narrates in detail the occasion on which Jesus gave the Spirit to the Church. ✻

THE LANCE-THRUST AND THE BURIAL

31 Because it was the eve of Passover, the Jews were anxious that the bodies should not remain on the cross for the coming Sabbath, since that Sabbath was a day of great solemnity; so they requested Pilate to have the legs broken
32 and the bodies taken down. The soldiers accordingly came to the first of his fellow-victims and to the second, and
33 broke their legs; but when they came to Jesus, they found that he was already dead, so they did not break his legs.
34 But one of the soldiers stabbed his side with a lance, and
35 at once there was a flow of blood and water. This is vouched for by an eyewitness, whose evidence is to be trusted. He knows that he speaks the truth, so that you
36 too may believe; for this happened in fulfilment of the
37 text of Scripture: 'No bone of his shall be broken.' And another text says, 'They shall look on him whom they pierced.'

38 After that, Pilate was approached by Joseph of Arima-thaea, a disciple of Jesus, but a secret disciple for fear of the Jews, who asked to be allowed to remove the body of Jesus. Pilate gave the permission; so Joseph came and took
39 the body away. He was joined by Nicodemus (the man who had first visited Jesus by night), who brought with him a mixture of myrrh and aloes, more than half a

hundredweight. They took the body of Jesus and wrapped 40
it, with the spices, in strips of linen cloth according to
Jewish burial-customs. Now at the place where he had 41
been crucified there was a garden, and in the garden a new
tomb, not yet used for burial. There, because the tomb 42
was near at hand and it was the eve of the Jewish Sabbath,
they laid Jesus.

✻ Usually the Romans allowed crucified bodies to rot away
on their crosses as a grim warning to all potential criminals.
But the Mosaic Law (Deut. 21: 23) ordained of a hanged man:
'his body shall not remain all night upon the tree, but thou
shalt surely bury him the same day, for he that is hanged is
accursed of God'. In this case the matter was specially urgent
because this particular night was the beginning both of the
Sabbath and of the first and great day of the Passover feast—
a day of great solemnity. Revolting as it sounds, the breaking of
crucified men's legs with a mallet was really an act of mercy
since it hastened death. In Jesus' case it was not needed. The
lance-thrust into his side, doubtless an attempt to ensure that
he was dead, produced, says John, *a flow of blood and water*.
He thought the detail significant and documented it (verse 35)
with an eyewitness's testimony. Why? He wished, say some,
to insist, as against some heretics, that Jesus really died—his
death was no mere semblance. Yet he probably saw in the
effusion a deeper meaning. For John, water and blood (both
in the Gospel and First Letter) are symbols of the salvation
Jesus brings—eternal life. John is then telling us, in his own
way, that the virtue of Christian salvation flows from the
completed sacrifice of the Son of God. Toplady's familiar
lines may well be true to John's meaning:

> Let the water and the blood
> From thy riven side which flowed
> Be of sin the double cure,
> Cleanse me from its guilt and power.

The effusion, we learn, is *vouched for by an eyewitness, whose evidence is to be trusted. He knows that he speaks the truth, so that you too may believe* (verse 35). Who is this witness? Since verse 26 records that the Beloved Disciple was present, it is probably he; and the whole verse is the evangelist's comment. All this, John concludes, happened in accordance with Scripture.

All the evangelists tell the story of the burial (verses 38–42), but John has his own quota of fresh details: the presence of Nicodemus, the elaborate embalming, the allusion to the garden, the nearness of the tomb to Golgotha.

The act of *Joseph of Arimathaea* (Ramathaim, 60 miles from Jerusalem), who was a member of the Sanhedrin (Mark 15: 43), showed high moral courage and nerved the rabbi *Nicodemus* to co-operate. Thus the last rites were rendered by two Jewish aristocrats who had never openly avowed themselves followers of Jesus. *More than half a hundredweight* of unguent seems an excessive amount for the purpose; but we read of a Gentile convert to Judaism who burned eighty pounds of spices at the death of Gamaliel the Elder. John is careful to point out (verse 40), perhaps for Gentile readers, that Jesus was embalmed (as Lazarus was) in the Jewish way which, unlike the Egyptian, involved no mutilation of the body. The unused tomb (verse 41), also mentioned by Matthew and Luke, in which the two friends laid Jesus' body, was presumably Joseph's own property and employed because the imminence of the Sabbath left no time to bury the body elsewhere.

36 f.   The first scripture is either Ps. 34: 40 or Exod. 12: 46. If it is the latter, John may be identifying Jesus with the paschal lamb (1 Cor. 5: 7). The second is taken from Zech. 12: 10. It is reasonable to hold that facts caused the discovery of the prophecies, and not vice versa. *

THE DAWN

✳ William Temple wrote: 'The date of the triumph of Jesus is Good Friday, not Easter Day. Yet if the story had ended there, the victory would have been barren. What remains is not to win it, but to gather in its fruits. Consequently St. John does not present the Resurrection as a mighty act by which the hosts of evil are routed but rather as the quiet rising of the sun which has already vanquished night. The atmosphere of the story has all the sweet freshness of dawn on a spring day.' ✳

THE EMPTY TOMB

Early on the Sunday morning, while it was still dark, **20** Mary of Magdala came to the tomb. She saw that the stone had been moved away from the entrance, and ran to 2 Simon Peter and the other disciple, the one whom Jesus loved. 'They have taken the Lord out of his tomb,' she cried, 'and we do not know where they have laid him.' So Peter and the other set out and made their way to the 3 tomb. They were running side by side, but the other 4 disciple outran Peter and reached the tomb first. He 5 peered in and saw the linen wrappings lying there, but did not enter. Then Simon Peter came up, following him, 6 and he went into the tomb. He saw the linen wrappings lying, and the napkin which had been over his head, not 7 lying with the wrappings but rolled together in a place by itself. Then the disciple who had reached the tomb first 8 went in too, and he saw and believed; until then they had 9 not understood the scriptures, which showed that he must rise from the dead.

✳ For John the fact of the empty tomb is of cardinal importance. He tells us not only how Mary Magdalene visited the grave, but how Peter and the Beloved Disciple did so also and assured themselves both of its emptiness and the state of the grave-clothes. The whole narrative has the ring of truth: behind it surely must lie the memory of an eyewitness.

Early on the Sunday morning, while it was still dark, i.e. between 3 and 6 a.m., Mary Magdalene makes her way to Joseph's rock-tomb to render the last offices of love, only to find the circular stone removed from the tomb's mouth. This at once makes her suspect that the tomb has been violated (tomb-rifling was not uncommon), and she hurries back to tell Peter and the Beloved Disciple. '*They have taken the Lord out of his tomb,*' she cried, '*and we do not know where they have laid him.*' Note the *we*, implying the presence of other women, as in the Synoptics (e.g. Mark 16: 1). This news sets the two disciples on a neck-and-neck race to the garden. The Beloved Disciple, probably because he was the younger man, outruns Peter to reach the tomb first and peer in at the linen wrappings on its floor. Peter, hard on his heels, goes further—he goes in. But for the moment he fails to grasp the meaning of the sight which meets his eyes: *the linen wrappings lying, and the napkin which had been over his head, not lying with the wrappings but rolled together in a place by itself.* Observe how careful is the description of the undisturbed grave-clothes. If the tomb had been hastily rifled, all would have been in confusion—thieves do not usually take time to tidy up. Had the disciples removed the body—a story which the Jews were soon to put around—the wrappings must have gone with the body. Instead, the evidence implied the miraculous—resurrection. The napkin, 'twirled up' like a turban, just as it had been wrapped round his head, lay there by itself, separate from the clothes. In short, the wording suggests that Jesus' physical body had passed, out of its wrappings, into what Paul called a 'spiritual' and glorified body, without deranging the grave-clothes which had lapsed back into their original places.

When the Beloved Disciple himself enters the tomb (verse 8), he divines at once what has happened and believes—believes that Jesus is risen. This is the true climax of the narrative. The evangelist adds a note that the scripture proof of the Resurrection came later. It was the experience of that Sunday which first brought conviction. For John it is only after the Resurrection that the scriptures illuminate the historical facts about Jesus.

No one saw Jesus rise. It is a miracle shrouded in mystery whose secret is known only to God. But, as David S. Cairns said, if the Resurrection is the land where the great mists lie, it is also the land where the great rivers spring. ∗

THE APPEARANCE TO MARY

So the disciples went home again; but Mary stood at the tomb outside, weeping. As she wept, she peered into the tomb; and she saw two angels in white sitting there, one at the head, and one at the feet, where the body of Jesus had lain. They said to her, 'Why are you weeping?' She answered, 'They have taken my Lord away, and I do not know where they have laid him.' With these words she turned round and saw Jesus standing there, but did not recognize him. Jesus said to her, 'Why are you weeping? Who is it you are looking for?' Thinking it was the gardener, she said, 'If it is you, sir, who removed him, tell me where you have laid him, and I will take him away.' Jesus said, 'Mary!' She turned to him and said, 'Rabbuni!' (which is Hebrew for 'My Master'). Jesus said, 'Do not cling to me, for I have not yet ascended to the Father. But go to my brothers, and tell them that I am now ascending to my Father and your Father, my God and your God.' Mary of Magdala went to the disciples with her news: 'I have seen the Lord!' she said, and gave them his message.

✱ This is 'the most humanly moving of all the stories of the risen Christ' (Dodd).

It was not to the disciples but to a woman, Mary of Magdala, who had stood at the cross and discovered the empty tomb that Jesus first appeared. Evidently she had followed the two disciples back to the tomb. Now, in tears, she *peered into* it and saw two angels. (Mark speaks of 'a youth', Matthew of one angel, Luke of two men. Whatever we make of them, they are 'witnesses to the mystery of the Resurrection'.) Her thoughts are still full of the 'removal' of the body when suddenly, turning round, she sees someone whom, in the dim light, she takes to be the gardener. When she asks him for information about the body, she is thrilled beyond all telling to hear her own name uttered in a voice she recognizes instantly: '*Mary!*' It is the greatest recognition scene in history —epitomized in two words. *Rabbuni*, an Aramaic word, is, we are told, a stronger form than *rabbi* and means 'My Lord'. Since in Jewish literature it is a title generally reserved for the *Divine* Lord, we may have here a confession of faith comparable to the coming one by Thomas.

At this point we must suppose Mary trying to clasp Jesus. Perhaps she wished to do him homage. Perhaps it was simply her woman's impulse, 'I will never let you go again'. He says, *Do not cling to me, for I have not yet ascended to the Father. But go to my brothers, and tell them that I am now ascending to my Father and your Father, my God and your God.* Jesus preserves the distinction (in relation to God) between himself and the disciples: he says 'my Father' and 'your Father', not 'our Father'. But it is the words which precede these which are mysterious. They evidently imply *an interim period* between Resurrection and Ascension. 'Stop clinging to me', says Jesus to Mary. He has not yet left the earth, so she need not fear he will disappear if she looses her grip. Yet he implies that the abiding possession of himself which she desires will soon be possible—after his Ascension. One week later, we find Thomas being invited to do the very thing forbidden to

Mary. It follows that, in John's view, Christ's ascension to the Father occurred in the interval—an inference confirmed by Christ's gift of the Spirit on the first Easter evening, for the Spirit was not to be given until Jesus was glorified (John 7: 39; 16: 7).

The scene closes with Mary hastening away, with her glad news, to fulfil Jesus' commission: *Go to my brothers, and tell them that I am now ascending* (or 'about to ascend'). The New Order is imminent—that New Order of the Spirit, in which Christ will be with his followers in a quite new way. ✶

THE APPEARANCE TO THE DISCIPLES

Late that Sunday evening, when the disciples were to- 19 gether behind locked doors, for fear of the Jews, Jesus came and stood among them. 'Peace be with you!' he said, and then showed them his hands and his side. So 20 when the disciples saw the Lord, they were filled with joy. Jesus repeated, 'Peace be with you!', and then said, 21 'As the Father sent me, so I send you.' He then breathed 22 on them, saying, 'Receive the Holy Spirit! If you forgive 23 any man's sins, they stand forgiven; if you pronounce them unforgiven, unforgiven they remain.'

✶ This narrative of the first Easter Sunday evening, which is independent of Luke's (Luke 24: 33–49), is so told as to show how events fulfilled promises made in chapters 14–17. Thus—

Jesus came (19)	I am coming back to you (14: 18)
Peace be with you (19)	Peace is my parting gift to you (14: 27)
They were filled with joy (20*b*)	Then you will be joyful (16: 22)

As the Father sent me, so I send you (21)	As thou hast sent me...I have sent them (17: 18)
Receive the Holy Spirit (22)	If I go, I will send him [the Spirit] to you (16: 7)

Ten disciples (Judas and Thomas were missing) must have been present, *behind locked doors*, on that first Easter evening when *Jesus came and stood among them*. Clearly his body was now free from some of its former limitations. His greeting is the conventional Jewish one. But, as has been said, a great man can redeem the conventional word from triviality and turn it into something for ever memorable and enheartening. It was to prove his identity that Jesus then *showed them his hands and his side*. His body, however spiritualized, was still the body which had hung on the cross. Next, with another *Peace* he commissioned his men: *As the Father sent me, so I send you*. As at the Last Supper the Twelve sat as representatives of the new Israel, the Church, so it was now with the Ten. Then followed their consecration. As Jesus *breathed on them*, suggesting that his very own spirit was being imparted to them, he said, *Receive the Holy Spirit*. The words recall Gen. 2: 7, 'The Lord God...breathed into his nostrils the breath of life'. This is the beginning of what Paul calls 'the new creation'. God the Redeemer now gives men the saving breath of the new life, which is the Holy Spirit, 'the Lord the Life-giver'.

The fact that it was on the first Easter day, according to John, that Jesus gave the Holy Spirit, has perplexed many. The story reads like 'a Johannine Pentecost'. How to reconcile it with the narrative in Acts 2 is the problem. And yet is it not psychologically probable that there should have been a time of waiting after the initial bestowal of the Spirit—a time when the Spirit worked among the apostles, like yeast in dough, until it burst forth on the day of Pentecost in a mighty release of divine power?

As Jesus breathes the Spirit upon the apostles, he empowers

them to represent him in dealing with sinners. Through them he commissions his Church of which they are the nucleus: *If you forgive any man's sins, they stand forgiven; if you pronounce them unforgiven, unforgiven they remain.* To his Church, then, as the Fellowship of the Spirit (cf. Phil. 2: 1), Christ gives the authority to pardon, or not to pardon. But only in so far as his Church, through its members, fulfils the condition, *Receive the Holy Spirit*, can this authority be properly exercised. ✶

THE APPEARANCE TO THOMAS

One of the Twelve, Thomas, that is 'the Twin', was not with the rest when Jesus came. So the disciples told him, 'We have seen the Lord.' He said, 'Unless I see the mark of the nails on his hands, unless I put my finger into the place where the nails were, and my hand into his side, I will not believe it.'

A week later his disciples were again in the room, and Thomas was with them. Although the doors were locked, Jesus came and stood among them, saying, 'Peace be with you!' Then he said to Thomas, 'Reach your finger here: see my hands; reach your hand here and put it into my side; be unbelieving no longer, but believe.' Thomas said, 'My Lord and my God!' Jesus said, 'Because you have seen me you have found faith. Happy are they who never saw me and yet have found faith.'

✶ In John's Gospel Thomas appears not so much as an out-and-out doubter as the type of those who demand tangible proof of what they are to believe as Christians. That he was completely loyal to Jesus, 11: 16 and 14: 5 prove. But he was literal-minded and demanded certainty as a condition of his self-committal. Wanting to believe, he was held back by fear of disillusionment.

It was *a week later*, again on a Sunday evening, that his great moment came. Again Jesus appeared in the room with locked doors and clothed his invitation to doubting Thomas in the words Thomas had used to voice his doubt. We are not actually told that Thomas touched Jesus. Perhaps Jesus meant, 'Put your hand in my side, if you still think such a test is needed'. At a single bound Thomas rose from the lowest depths of faith to its very pinnacle: *My Lord and my God! My Lord*, the familiar title given to Jesus in the days of his flesh; *my God*, the title of Deity. It is as if (said Burkitt) Thomas said, 'Yes, it is Jesus—and he is Divine!' We recall 1:1: *And what God was, the Word was.* The wheel of the Gospel has come full circle. The note struck in the beginning rings out in its ending. John's testimony to the life of Jesus is meant to lead men to precisely this confession of Jesus: *my Lord and my God*.

But the last word is the Lord's: *Because you have seen me you have found faith. Happy are they who never saw me and yet have found faith.* The walls of that room with the locked doors fall away. From this moment the company of the eleven disciples begins to grow, to expand, to take in everyone who in every age and clime has faith and includes himself in the final beatitude of Jesus. True faith in the risen Lord is not really based on the evidence of physical eye or ear but on experience, attested by thousands upon thousands down the centuries, of those who have testified, 'Christ is alive, and I have known the secret of his Presence'. *

CONCLUSION

30 There were indeed many other signs that Jesus performed in the presence of his disciples, which are not
31 recorded in this book. Those here written have been recorded in order that you may hold the faith that Jesus is the Christ, the Son of God, and that through this faith you may possess eternal life by his name.

✶ Many scholars believe John meant to end his Gospel here and call chapter 21 an epilogue or appendix. This is by no means certain, as the introduction to chapter 21 will show.

John tells us that he could have recorded many more *signs* of Jesus. Those he has recorded he has chosen for a deliberate purpose, to evoke and foster saving faith in Jesus as the Messiah and the Son of God, so that his readers (in the first instance, people in Ephesus, but the words extend to all later readers) may have that *eternal life* which is God's gift to men in his Son. ✶

ENVOY

✶ Before we come to the text, we must discuss two questions raised by this chapter:

1. *Is it an Appendix?*

Because 20: 31 reads like the end of the Gospel, it has become fashionable to call chapter 21 'The Appendix to the Fourth Gospel' and to regard it as an afterthought. Some have even thought it the work of another hand. Yet there is no manuscript evidence for this, nor does a study of the style compel such a conclusion. We may therefore hold that it comes from the same hand as wrote chapters 1–20.

But is 'Appendix' a just description? Consider only two points. (1) We find precisely the same literary phenomenon in 1 John 5: 13 as we find in the Gospel at 20: 31. John writes what looks like a concluding sentence—yet the letter goes on for seven more verses. It looks as if John had a way of practically writing *finis* and then adding a bit more before he ended. (2) A Gospel, as we know it, does not end simply with an appearance, or appearances, of the risen Lord. It always includes his commissioning of his disciples for their future work. John 21 is such a commission.

'Envoy' (which means a sending on one's way) would therefore be a better word than 'Appendix' to describe this last chapter.

2. *What is its purpose?*

One reply might be: to tell another and vivid story of the risen Lord. But this is certainly not the whole answer. Accordingly, some have held that it was added to clear up a misunderstanding about the Beloved Disciple's destiny. A prophecy was current (see verse 23) that Jesus had promised to return before all his disciples died. Yet the last of them, the Beloved Disciple, had apparently died, and the prophecy looked like being falsified. So the evangelist clarifies what Jesus really said (verse 22). But it is also probable that he wished to indicate the very different work which their Lord designed for Peter and for the Beloved Disciple. In this Gospel the Beloved Disciple (whom we take to be John the Apostle) is depicted as the apostle of insight *par excellence* (see 13: 23–6; 20: 10; 21: 7), whereas Peter is the man of action. Therefore in chapter 21 the practical oversight of the flock is given to Peter ('Feed my sheep'); whereas the Beloved Disciple's task is to be theological, rather than pastoral. He is to be the witness and guardian of the Lord's revelation and the truth of the Gospel. And such in fact he became by his testimony which is enshrined in the Gospel of John. ✶

THE RISEN LORD BY THE LAKE

21 Some time later, Jesus showed himself to his disciples
2 once again, by the Sea of Tiberias; and in this way. Simon Peter and Thomas 'the Twin' were together with Nathanael of Cana-in-Galilee. The sons of Zebedee and two
3 other disciples were also there. Simon Peter said, 'I am going out fishing.' 'We will go with you', said the others. So they started and got into the boat. But that night they caught nothing.
4 Morning came, and there stood Jesus on the beach, but

the disciples did not know that it was Jesus. He called out 5
to them, 'Friends, have you caught anything?' They
answered 'No.' He said, 'Shoot the net to starboard, and 6
you will make a catch.' They did so, and found they could
not haul the net aboard, there were so many fish in it.
Then the disciple whom Jesus loved said to Peter, 'It is the 7
Lord!' When Simon Peter heard that, he wrapped his
coat about him (for he had stripped) and plunged into the
sea. The rest of them came on in the boat, towing the net 8
full of fish; for they were not far from land, only about a
hundred yards.

When they came ashore, they saw a charcoal fire there, 9
with fish laid on it, and some bread. Jesus said, 'Bring 10
some of your catch.' Simon Peter went aboard and 11
dragged the net to land, full of big fish, a hundred and
fifty-three of them; and yet, many as they were, the net
was not torn. Jesus said, 'Come and have breakfast.' None 12
of the disciples dared to ask 'Who are you?' They knew
it was the Lord. Jesus now came up, took the bread, and 13
gave it to them, and the fish in the same way.

This makes the third time that Jesus appeared to his 14
disciples after his resurrection from the dead.

* There are several striking similarities between this story and
Luke 5: 1–11. To be sure, there are also differences—in Luke
there are two boats, and the nets are torn. Is it possible that
Luke's narrative is in fact another version of John's story of the
risen Christ by the lake? Certainly Peter's words in Luke 5: 8,
'Go, Lord, leave me sinner that I am' might have been uttered
by the thrice-denying Peter to his risen Lord.

1. *Jesus showed himself.* The risen Lord was not continuously
visible after the Resurrection.

by the Sea of Tiberias: alias the Lake of Galilee. See 6: 1.

2. Seven disciples: Peter and Thomas, Nathanael, James and John plus an anonymous two. Only here in the Gospel are *the sons of Zebedee* mentioned.

I am going out fishing. The remark of a man of action to whom, during the time of waiting, it was torture to be idle.

3. *that night they caught nothing.* Night was the best time for fishing.

4 f. Let Ruskin paint the picture: 'But when the morning came, in the clear light of it, behold a figure stood on the shore. They were not thinking of anything but their fruitless hauls. They had no guess who it was. It asked them simply if they had caught anything. They said no; and it tells them to cast yet again. And John shades his eyes from the morning sun with his hand, to look who it is: and though the glinting of the sea, too, dazzles him, he makes out who it is, at last; and poor Simon, not to be outrun this time, tightens his fisher's coat about him, and dashes in, over the nets. One would have liked to see him swim those hundred yards, and stagger to his knees on the beach.'

6. *Shoot the net to starboard, and you will make a catch.* A command so definite must indicate knowledge, wherever it came from. There is no need to find anything miraculous or symbolic here. The Lake of Galilee swarmed then, as it still does, with fish. Jesus had evidently noticed a large shoal.

7. The Beloved Disciple is the first to recognize the stranger; Peter the first to act. He pulls on his fisherman's jacket, *for he had stripped* for rowing, i.e. was naked save for his loin-cloth, and plunges into the waves.

9 f. A *fire, fish, bread.* Jesus had prepared a simple meal; and when the seven arrived, invited them to join him and to pool their resources.

11. *a hundred and fifty-three of them.* Down the centuries commentators have had a great time with the number. The best of a bad lot of guesses is that, since ancient zoologists counted 153 different species of fish, the catch symbolizes the universality of the Gospel. Calvin, with his usual sense, warns us

against making 'a sublime mystery' out of the number. In our view, the 153 fish are no more symbolical than the hundred yards that Peter swam. It is the remembered number of a 'bumper' catch.

13. Jesus acted as host; and what he did recalled his actions at the Last Supper. *

THE REINSTATEMENT OF PETER

After breakfast, Jesus said to Simon Peter, 'Simon son of 15 John, do you love me more than all else?' 'Yes, Lord,' he answered, 'you know that I love you.' 'Then feed my lambs', he said. A second time he asked, 'Simon son of 16 John, do you love me?' 'Yes, Lord, you know I love you.' 'Then tend my sheep.' A third time he said, 'Simon 17 son of John, do you love me?' Peter was hurt that he asked him a third time, 'Do you love me?' 'Lord,' he said, 'you know everything; you know I love you.' Jesus said, 'Feed my sheep.

'And further, I tell you this in very truth: when you 18 were young you fastened your belt about you and walked where you chose; but when you are old you will stretch out your arms, and a stranger will bind you fast, and carry you where you have no wish to go.' He said this to 19 indicate the manner of death by which Peter was to glorify God. Then he added, 'Follow me.'

* Peter had denied Jesus three times. Now, with a threefold question he is reinstated. Some scholars hold that John 21 contains the substance of the lost end of Mark. Now in Mark 16: 7 the 'youth' by the empty tomb bids the women 'give this message to his disciples and Peter: "He will go on before you into Galilee and you will see him there, as he told you"'

This suggests the Lord's special concern for Peter. John tells how, when they met again, the denier was movingly forgiven and recommissioned for service.

The dialogue between Jesus and Peter contains two different Greek verbs for loving: *agapan*: 'love'; and *philein*: 'be a friend to'. The N.E.B.—not without very good reason, for John is demonstrably fond of synonyms—renders both verbs alike by 'love'. Yet it remains just possible (as the N.E.B.'s footnote allows) that John is contrasting the two verbs, *agapan* expressing the higher Christian love, and *philein* simple human friendship. Thus (1) Jesus: 'Do you love me?' Peter: 'You know that I am your friend.' (2) Jesus: 'Do you love me?' Peter: 'You know I am your friend.' (3) Jesus: 'Are you my friend?' Peter: 'You know everything; you know I am your friend.'

15. *do you love me more than all else?* Literally, 'Do you love me more than these?' 'These' might refer to the boats and the nets and the old life. More probably it refers to the other disciples. Peter had protested that his loyalty was greater than theirs (John 13: 37; Mark 14: 29).

Then feed my lambs. Peter's commission is pastoral. 1 Peter 5: 2-4 records how he passed on his commission to others in the name of the 'Head Shepherd' of the Flock.

17. *A third time he said.* The one question had to be put three times because love to Christ is the one thing essential for the ministry to which Peter—and all true pastors—are called.

18. The interpretation of this verse is shaped by the following one where John explains that Jesus was hinting at Peter's coming martyrdom. Yet the words of Jesus primarily describe the helplessness of old age in contrast with the confident freedom of youth. Thus *you will stretch out your arms* suggests the helpless lifting up of an old man's arms to let another clothe him.

19. The evangelist's comment which probably indicates that Peter had in fact died like his Master by crucifixion.

Follow me. Peter evidently took this command quite

literally, but the words would recall his first summons to follow Christ. *

THE DESTINY OF THE BELOVED DISCIPLE

Peter looked round, and saw the disciple whom Jesus 20 loved following—the one who at supper had leaned back close to him to ask the question, 'Lord, who is it that will betray you?' When he caught sight of him, Peter asked, 21 'Lord, what will happen to him?' Jesus said, 'If it should 22 be my will that he wait until I come, what is it to you? Follow me.'

That saying of Jesus became current in the brotherhood, 23 and was taken to mean that that disciple would not die. But in fact Jesus did not say that he would not die; he only said, 'If it should be my will that he wait until I come, what is it to you?'

* 20 f. As Peter moves to follow Jesus, the Beloved Disciple moves also. Peter's curiosity is aroused. His own destiny has been foretold. What about the Beloved Disciple's? Jesus rebukes Peter: if it is his will that the Beloved Disciple should survive till he comes, this is no business of Peter's.

23. The evangelist explains that a rumour current in the Church said, on Christ's authority, that the Beloved Disciple would survive till Christ's coming. Nothing so precise, comments the evangelist, had in fact been said. All he had said was, 'What if...'.

The doctrine of Christ's coming implied here is more like 1 John 2: 28 than anything else in the Gospel. Evidently there was some alleged saying of Jesus current in the Church which was misunderstood to mean that the venerable disciple would survive till Christ's Second Advent. It is a fair inference that verse 23 was written after the disciple's death, to remove any misunderstanding. *

POSTSCRIPT

24 It is this same disciple who attests what has here been written. It is in fact he who wrote it, and we know that his testimony is true.

25   There is much else that Jesus did. If it were all to be recorded in detail, I suppose the whole world would not hold the books that would be written.

✳ Verse 24 reads like a certificate written by the elders of the Ephesian Church to testify to the evangelist's veracity. (Was it written during his lifetime or after his death?) It declares that the Beloved Disciple's testimony lies behind the Gospel, and that, whether directly or mediately—for the Greek might mean 'caused to be written', as in 19: 19—he was its author. The Muratorian Canon, a Christian document going back to about A.D. 180, says that others encouraged John the disciple to write his Gospel and assisted him.

    Verse 25 ends the book with a magnificent hyperbole. The Gospel contains only a selection of Jesus' deeds. To tell the complete story of the *deeds of Christ* would tax the world's capacity. So in our time T. R. Glover has said: 'The Gospels are not four but ten thousand times ten thousand and thousands of thousands, and the last word of every one of them is, "Lo, I am with you alway, even unto the end of the world".' ✳

✳   ✳   ✳   ✳   ✳   ✳   ✳   ✳   ✳   ✳   ✳   ✳

An Incident in the Temple

AND THEY WENT each to his home, and Jesus to the 53, 1
Mount of Olives. At daybreak he appeared again in 2
the temple, and all the people gathered round him. He
had taken his seat and was engaged in teaching them
when the doctors of the law and the Pharisees brought in a 3
woman detected in adultery. Making her stand out in the
middle they said to him, 'Master, this woman was caught 4
in the very act of adultery. In the Law Moses has laid 5
down that such women are to be stoned. What do you
say about it?' They put the question as a test, hoping to 6
frame a charge against him. Jesus bent down and wrote
with his finger on the ground. When they continued to 7
press their question he sat up straight and said, 'That one
of you who is faultless shall throw the first stone.' Then 8
once again he bent down and wrote on the ground. When 9
they heard what he said, one by one they went away, the
eldest first; and Jesus was left alone, with the woman still
standing there. Jesus again sat up and said to the woman, 10
'Where are they? Has no one condemned you?' 'No 11
one, sir', she said. Jesus replied, 'No more do I. You may
go; do not sin again.'

* Two things seem certain: (1) This is a true story about
Jesus; and (2) it is not a true part of John's Gospel.

The case against its traditional place in John at 7: 53 is
threefold:

(*a*) The passage does not occur at all in many of our oldest
and best manuscripts.

(*b*) Its style and vocabulary resemble that of the earlier Gospels, especially Luke. (This point is clearer in the original Greek.)

(*c*) In its traditional place it breaks the sequence of the narrative.

The manuscripts which have the passage put it in various places: some after Luke 21: 38, others after John 7: 36, 7: 52 or 21: 24.

Evidently the story about Jesus and the adulteress was handed down orally in the Church; but, because its teaching seemed to encourage lax treatment of sinners, it failed to win a place in the canonical scriptures. Later, when church discipline grew less severe, it returned to favour—and a place in the Gospels. For this we may well be grateful: few stories are more authentically stamped with 'Christ's touch'.

To understand it, we should remember two points: (1) it is the story of a trap that did not come off; and (2) Jesus is here, ironically, playing the part of Roman judge.

the doctors of the law and the Pharisees are here laying the same kind of trap as the Pharisees and Herodians sought to lay in their question about the tribute money (Mark 12: 13–17). If Jesus sanctions the execution of the woman, he usurps the power of Rome who alone could inflict capital punishment. If he forbids it, he contravenes the Law of Moses. But note how Jesus evades the dilemma. He writes in the dust. This writing accords with the procedures of Roman criminal law: the presiding judge would first write down the sentence on a tablet and then read it aloud. (T. W. Manson, to whom we owe this insight, cites examples of this practice.) Thus Jesus by his action says in effect: 'You are inviting me to usurp the functions of the Roman Governor. Very well, I will do so and in the approved Roman way.' He stoops and pretends to write down the sentence, after which he reads it out: *That one of you who is faultless shall throw the first stone.* It is a masterstroke of mercy seasoning justice. Jesus defeats the plotters by going through the form of passing sentence in the best Roman style, but at the same time so wording it that it cannot be carried out.

Yet Christ's mercy is not laxity. His last word to the woman when her accusers have slunk away, neither condemns nor condones. It bids her forsake her former way of life: *You may go; do not sin again.*

5. For the Mosaic Law about a detected adulteress see Lev. 20: 10 and Deut. 22: 21 ff. Evidently death by stoning was ordered only in the case of a betrothed virgin. ✶

✶   ✶   ✶   ✶   ✶   ✶   ✶   ✶   ✶   ✶   ✶   ✶   ✶

INDEX OF NAMES AND TOPICS

The references are to pages

INDEX OF NAMES AND TOPICS